THIS BOOK BELONGS TO THE LIBRARY OF

Paul and Mary Hansen
33 Mohawk Drive
Blackhawk Heights
Illinois

April 1951

JOHANN WOLFGANG VON GOETHE

FAUST

A TRAGEDY: IN A MODERN TRANSLATION BY ALICE RAPHAEL

Illustrated with eighteen lithographs by

EUGENE DELACROIX

NEW YORK : THE HERITAGE PRESS

CONTENTS

INTRODUCTION

BY CARL F. SCHREIBER

TOWARD NOON on March twenty-second, 1832, Goethe closed his eyes forever on a world which he was privileged to understand as few human beings have been permitted to know it. For a period of eighty-two years those eyes "Zum Sehen geboren, zum Schauen bestellt" had observed the objects of this earth with a profound reverence; they had peered into the mysteries of human existence with a hope of solving the imponderables that hold the lives of men enmeshed. Goethe's genius preserved, even in old age, a childlike wonderment and an untrammeled vision to a phenomenal degree. His reverence for all forms of life is a definite mark of his genius. "What a glorious, precious thing is every living organism! How suited to its condition, how genuine!" And the chief guide to Goethe's universal understanding was the eye, "that noblest of all the senses." Whatever else Goethe was, he was first and foremost a devoted observer. To Homer and to Milton sight was not a chief requisite. Their works are largely imaginative; with their mind's eye, they created a world of glorious fiction. Goethe was a seer.

In a very real sense Goethe was a prophet. He did not divine by observing the entrails of birds, or their flight. His promises, premonitions, and his faith were based on more reliable observations. The earth and its living forces, society and its traditions and conventions: from these two primal sources, Goethe amassed the wisdom for which he has become so justly famous.

Of this wisdom, of this understanding, Goethe's greatest masterpiece, the "Faust", received a major share. It beats with the living heart of the world. Fully sixty years had elapsed between the inception of the "Faust" and the completion of the Second Part. All the thrill of the will to accomplish and succeed is chronicled in his Diaries during the months of June, July and August, 1831. Time and again the entry: Haeptzweck or Hauptgeschäft! There can be no dallying now. On his 82nd birthday the "Faust" must reach completion. No indisposition, no private worries must interfere with the Hauptzweck. On July 22nd, Goethe could write that his main purpose had now been accomplished. However, the motifs of the "Faust" continued to hum on in his mind. At the end of January of the next year, Goethe once more addresses himself to an expansion of several themes which he had treated too briefly in order to finish within the time-limit set by himself. Then the manuscript is sealed up and laid away. It appeared late in 1832 as the first in the series of Goethe's posthumous writings.

It can be no part of an introduction to the translation of the First Part of "Faust" to discuss the Goethean plan of man's salvation. The grand purpose of the "Faust" is only faintly indicated in Part I. Not until Part II does Goethe entrust the reader with the key to "Faust's" salvation:

> Gerettet ist das edle Glied
> Der Geisterwelt vom Bösen:
> "Wer immer strebend sich bemüht,
> Den können wir erlösen".
> Und hat an ihm die Liebe gar
> Von oben teilgenommen,
> Begegnet ihm die selige Schar
> Mit herzlichem Willkommen.

A word of caution is the purpose of these brief remarks. To interrupt the "Faust" at the conclusion of Part One, is an injustice which has far too often been done Goethe. The two parts of "Faust" stand in a similar relation to each other, as do the Old and the New Testaments. The one heralds a promise, is quickened by anticipation; the other chronicles the fulfilment of the covenant.

The "Faust" theme is as old as that first concept which gave the urge to utter the earliest expression for wizard. It was born and nurtured in an atmosphere of discontent with the neutral limits set for man. It savors of conjuration and smacks of doom. Pronounce the word Faustus, and the lid to Pandora's box lifts itself and out scramble a horde of eerie personages: Virgilius and Merlin, the two friars Bacon and Bungay, Theophilus, too, along with Robert the Devil and the Duke of Luxemburg; then Don Juan in the company of the Dutch Mariken van Nymwegen and the Polish Twardowski. Even Ahasuerus, the Wandering Jew, has a decided inclination to respond to this magic word. The "Faust" theme has an astonishing range, both mentally and geographically. It has held most of the nations of the western world within its spell. The historical Dr. Faustus was a contemporary of Martin Luther. He called himself Faustus, Junior. Whether there ever existed a Faustus, Senior, from whom the younger man inherited his occult science is of no import. The designation was probably a potent factor in pushing the Faustian claims back into indeterminate time. Occultism thrives best in time and space with blurred edges. Fifty years after Faust had lived his damnable life and come to his tragic end, he had become a legend, a rapidly enlarging myth, a convenient rallying point for every type of anecdote or incident involving conjuration, hocus-pocus, and sleight-of-hand. In 1587 an anonymous writer published the first account of his life. The book seems to have sped on its way across the Channel, where it was Englished. "Kit" Marlowe found the material to his liking and moulded it into his immortal tragedy. English travelling players carried the drama back to German soil, where it seems to have enjoyed an unusual popularity. From which turgid spring the puppet-show of Dr. Faustus, an early rival of the legitimate drama, had its source is difficult to determine. It probably harks back to one of the many Faust books which succeeded the first. At all events there were now three popular channels through which the Faust theme ran steadily to Goethe's time: the drama, the puppet-show, and the chapbook.

As an old man Goethe remarked to von Müller that he had carried the plan of the "Faust" in his head as an untold tale (ein inneres Märchen) for many, many years (so vielen Jahren); how many is to scholars a moot question. If we are to believe Goethe (and I incline to the faith that the author is his own best witness) the date of inception was 1769, a year during which Goethe was steeping himself in the occult sciences and performing alchemistic experiments with Fräulein von Klettenberg. Certainly the constellations were in a proper conjunction at that period propitious to the birth of that tantalizingly subjective First Part of the "Faust". On another occasion Goethe sublimes his appraisal of the completed "Faust" in Eckermann's presence: "The First Part is almost entirely subjective; it is the product of a mind inhibited and highly emotional; an atmosphere of gloaming hovers over it, and it is for this reason that it proves so engaging to the majority of readers. In the Second Part there is almost nothing of a subjective nature. It reflects a loftier, more expansive, clearer, and a more dispassionate world, so that he who has not bestirred himself a bit and gathered some experience, will find it quite impossible to make anything of it."

I have no apologies to make when I seemingly demean the "Faust" by designating it as a text-book of human experience. Each of the many varying themes of the "Faust" is comparable to an experiment performed with care, founded on fact, and written up with supreme insight and grace. The Study, Mephisto's catechization of the student, Auerbach's Cellar, the Witch's Kitchen, the Brocken, the Imperial Diet, the Masquerade, the invention of paper money, the Laboratory, the Classical Walpurgisnacht, the Helena, are all independent spheres, closed incidents, which act and react on one another without suffering the slightest loss of entity. Of this conception of his "Faust" we have Goethe's own approval. "The chief requisite of my composition is this, that the separate divisions must each be significant and clear; as a whole the drama will always remain incommensurable. This has the advantage of an insoluble problem, which continuously entices the human mind to ever repeated attempts at solution." This method of composing often worked Goethe great hardships. It was his invariable practice to attack that portion of the greater work which attracted him at the moment (ihn anmutete). The last act of the "Tasso" was the first to be completed. In the Second Part of the "Faust", Act IV was the last to be finished. Goethe's genius rarely failed him in finding the significant transitions which are so indispensable to the proper evaluation of the completed work.

To put in other words, the "Faust" is Protean. It is constantly changing and shifting, both as to content and as to form. Its moods run the whole scale from deepest melancholy to that jubilant moment,

> "O stay! Thou art so fair!"

Its outer form embraces the most astonishing variants from the purest lyric to the doggerel; from the characteristically German free rhyme, to a passage left in prose. From every page of the "Faust" an unheard and unheeded voice seems to whisper: Translator, beware! Despite this warning at least forty-six English "Faust" translations have been published, of which number an appreciable majority are of Part One.

Englishmen, Irishmen, Scotchmen, and Americans have been lured by some strange urge to embark upon this perilous venture. "They come from many different walks and stations of life: educated and ignorant; rich and poor; socially and politically prominent, as well as the plain citizens and commoners"; some so obscure that they have left but this one sole trace of their existence. As they pass in silent review one recognizes the wealthy timber merchant, Jonathan Birch; the journalists and writers, Bayard Taylor and Lewis Filmore: the police magistrate, Thomas Arnold; the architect, W. B. Clarke; members of the civil service and soldiers, Captain Knox and G. M. Cookson; and the Pension Office clerk, Frank Claudy. The learned professions are well represented by the scientists, James Adey Birds and John Galvan; the law delegation is impressive with Abraham Hayward and Sir Theodore Martin; university professors and scholars comprise a larger group with John Anster, John Stuart Blackie, William H. Van der Smissen and Albert G. Latham; the physicians are William Bell Macdonald, Sir George William Lefevre, and John Todhunter; the representatives from the ranks of the clergy are Arthur Thompson Gurney, Charles Timothy Brooks, and Charles Kegan Paul; two women fittingly grace the ranks, Anna Swanwick and Alice Raphael. Finally Sir George Buchanan, the British Ambassador, the Honorable Robert Talbot, and Lord Francis Leveson-Gower, M.P., top the list as representatives of the highest social and political circles.

The roster of English "Faust" translators has purposely been drawn out to some length. It lends striking evidence to the appeal "Faust" has made to individuals in the various cultivated walks of life. Goethe's overmastering love of truth, his devotion to and glorification of the everyday things of life have insinuated themselves into the consciousness of men everywhere—but with a difference of degree, and especially with a wide range of interpretation. And if interpretation of a masterpiece is so vital to a reasoned understanding of the original, then it seems only proper that every translation should in and of itself reinterpret for a new generation the scenes which are rendered from one idiom into another. There is abundant evidence to assume that this principle underlies the great majority of attempts to English the "Faust". A comparison of the earliest versions with those of the middle range, and again with those of our own day will reflect a gradually evolving evaluation running the whole gamut from prejudice to forbearance and then with a marked acceleration to understanding and appreciation. A definite joy of emancipation must come over him who, with the requisite love, has translated the "Faust". Goethe looking back on his long literary career once remarked to von Müller: "Whoever has read my works with some care, must be willing to admit that he has attained to a certain spiritual freedom (innere Freiheit)."

To Alice Raphael, "Faust" is an experience, an event in her struggle for emancipation. Of her love for Goethe's inspired drama there can be no doubt. She has the mark of "Faust" upon her, for she felt her way into the spirit of the immortal poem, before she resorted to scholarship to convince herself that what she had experienced was not her creation, but a faithful portrayal of the Goethean "Faust".

TRANSLATOR'S FOREWORD

QUIET WORK

One lesson, Nature, let me learn of thee,
One lesson which in every wind is blown,
One lesson of two duties kept at one
Though the loud world proclaim their enmity—

Of toil unsever'd from tranquillity!
Of labour, that in lasting fruit outgrows
Far noisier schemes, accomplish'd in repose,
Too great for haste, too high for rivalry!

Yes, while on earth a thousand discords ring,
Man's fitful uproar mingling with his toil,
Still do thy sleepless ministers move on,

Their glorious tasks in silence perfecting;
Still working, blaming still our vain turmoil,
Labourers that shall not fail, when man is gone.

During the many years in which "Faust" has been my companion, this sonnet of Matthew Arnold's has become more and more closely associated with it. For the poem expresses the temper in which this translation has slowly evolved and also the spirit in which Goethe toiled to understand Nature, but to which he gave expression only in the Second Part of "Faust." The significance of Goethe's labour, which "in lasting fruit outgrows far noisier schemes", can be more clearly understood as we approach the hundredth year following his death than during his lifetime.

To-day every nation which bears the imprint of Western culture acknowledges Goethe's influence, and gradually the world has come to realize his pre-eminence as a human being, that he is in truth "the first full-statured man", as Bayard Taylor so happily expressed it. Goethe is so important to modern man because he struggled consciously and ceaselessly throughout his life to integrate the manifold aspects of his richly endowed personality under the hierarchy of his will; his conflicts were the struggles which lead to self-mastery, his aim the development of his possibilities, and his goal the conquest of his own nature.

There has come into existence a Goethe-world, and one of the happiest experiences of the past years has been the communicating and sharing of this translation with kindred spirits. To many friends my thanks are due who have shared the trials and tribulations of the Faustian pilgrimage.

It gives me great pleasure to acknowledge the assistance of Richard Bloch, whose lifelong study of "Faust" enabled him to render such signal service to the translation in its earlier stages, and of Alice Rodewald, whose scholarly criticism clarified many a problem in English prosody. But above all this translation is indebted to the late Professor William A. Speck of Yale University for his never failing aid and encouragement as the work emerged into its final form. Only because of his unsparing generosity and devotion to the exactness of the original have I been able to learn the lesson of "two duties kept at one", and to bring the art of the poet into harmony with the demands of the scholar. Under Professor Speck's guidance, in the quiet of the Goethe room, during many hours of "toil unsever'd from tranquillity", this translation slowly ripened into maturity and now stands as an acknowledgment to his labour of love.

A NOTE

BY MARK VAN DOREN

"People may say what they like of the inadequacy of translation, it is and it remains one of the weightiest and worthiest of employments in the general life of the world." So Goethe wrote to his young friend Carlyle, and so anyone will believe who takes a serious interest in poetry. Goethe was not one of those who hold that a good poem cannot be translated. He was nearer the opinion that only a good poem can be translated—only a poem, that is, which has the major virtue of saying something as well as the minor virtue of saying it in precious ways peculiar to the languages in which the poet wrote. He himself spent six decades of his life in writing such a poem, and many years have been spent by others in translating it into English. "Faust" can be translated. Whatever people may say of the inadequacy of the result, it remains that the result is one of the worthiest things a modern mind can undertake to achieve.

"Faust" not only can but should be translated, and the work should be done again and again and again, as indeed it has, for more than forty versions in English now exist. But there is the special necessity that it be done freshly for each new generation. An original poem has something in it which defies fashion; it is always more or less new and brightly strange. Versions of it in a foreign tongue, however, are likely to take on tarnish; the image needs regilding. So with the established English versions of "Faust"; having been made of course in the nineteenth century, they are distinguished by the very demerits which modern English and American poets have most deliberately avoided. Even Bayard Taylor's "Faust", standard as it once was, and energetic as it still is in so many places, wears the dust of Victorian idiom, Victorian inversion, Victorian rhetoric. Consequently his translation cannot be read with continuous pleasure by those who should read him at all, and this is a pity, since pleasure is what we have the right to expect from "Faust". It should be as easy to read as possible, with the minimum of reminders that what we hold in our hands is a translation—a translation which, if it has been done faithfully, has been done, as anyone familiar with the ground must know, with torturous labour.

Of the several versions of "Faust" which have appeared in the present century Alice Raphael's is, I think, the best in its combination of fidelity and form. Alice Raphael has not been content with the labour, great and important as it is, of rendering the whole and exact meaning of the original in every line. She has done that, and has had the benefit of consultation with scholars whenever she was in doubt as to what Goethe had meant to say. One scholar in particular gave generously of his great knowledge, making with the translator a most minute scrutiny of the original and insisting in every instance that the thought should not suffer. The late Mr. William A. Speck, of the Yale University Library, Goethe collector extraordinary, stood godfather to the present translation. But Alice Raphael has done more than test her accuracy at such a source. She has conceived it to be her duty to write a poem, and she has used all her knowledge of poetry, together with her skill in writing it, towards this end. She has wanted to give joy to her readers in something like the measure in which Goethe himself gave her joy—and with it understanding—from the time she first became acquainted with his masterpiece. The accomplishment of this purpose has been her chief occupation for a dozen years.

Her "Faust" as it now stands is far from being the poem which she first wrote. Like the original itself it has undergone a complicated process of growth, passing through four forms before it became what the reader possesses. In the beginning it was free verse—for the time was 1917, and free verse seemed to her at the moment the only fit vehicle for the communication of so strenuous and insistent a theme. Free verse in America was then at the height of its vogue. The vogue declined; Alice Raphael, like many another American poet, doubted its adequacy in the matters of harmony and emotion; and her "Faust" was rewritten in blank verse. After a few years it was written again, this time in better blank verse. Then, and finally, Alice Raphael discovered that she could not dispense after all with the original harmonies—rhyme, metre, and every other convention of which Goethe had made use. Such a decision came, she says, "not as the result of an intellectual compromise, but spontaneously out of an organic process of development." The poem grew into its completed form "out of a mature understanding of the problems involved in a true communication of Goethe." So we have a translation which, like many that preceded it, follows the original, rhyme by rhyme and metre by metre. The lines change their lengths as Goethe's did theirs, with very few exceptions. Upon occasion a quatrain has been rendered as two couplets, or two couplets as a quatrain; and feminine endings have every-where been discarded because the translator felt they were unsuitable to the genius of English prosody when put to the task of expressing Goethe. In general, however, the reader may be assured that he hears the poem as Goethe, standing on the other side of his interpreter, wanted him to hear it. There is a certain peril for most translators in thus enslaving themselves to the form of their originals, and Alice Raphael has found the limitation at times embarrassing. But no one should know better than she the rewards to be reaped by being faithful. Her return, after years of wander-ing, to the letter of Goethe is one of the profoundest compliments to him that I can imagine. It seems to vindicate him as a poet more completely than any idle gesture of reverence, or heedless resolve to echo his voice. And once more it brings up the question of the value we are to set on paraphrase. Paraphrase, it seems to me, will do well enough in most cases of translation, and in many cases will actually give us an improvement on the original; but where a masterpiece is under consideration there will be no escaping the form in which the master worked. A great poem says what it has to say not merely in words, in thoughts; it says it in quatrains, too, or songs, or triple rhymes; the form, in other words, may be indis-pensable to our understanding.

Alice Raphael spent a dozen years upon the text of her "Faust", but she has spent twice that many years with the poem itself. Her first reading of it, in 1906, was an experience of almost cataclysmic dimensions in her life. "Faust" literally flooded her consciousness, driving out for a time other poems and other ideas. And it held its ground, though she herself did not realize the extent to which it had done so until more than a decade had gone by. Then, at a crucial stage in her psychological development, she felt the domination of "Faust", even its tyranny, but saw the promise in it of some answer to her own problem, some discipline, some light upon the secret of life as that secret presented itself, darkly yet insistently, to her mind. Beginning with a few passages which she had felt impelled to put into English, she went quickly on to do the whole in a rapid draft. But the process had only begun. It was to take twelve years, and it was to be finished not as a flourish is finished but as a phase of life is brought to its solid end.

The mention of psychology in the present connection is almost inevitable in view of the attention which "Faust" has received from men like Jung and Freud. It is one of the many great human myths which they have explored in the course of their researches into the soul—and not the "Faust" legend merely, but that legend as Goethe in particular treated it. To an old and popular story Goethe brought the immense resources of his experience and imagination; in the innumerable subtleties of his poem, and in the wise inspiration of its imagery, a century in advance he led the way for scientists of the soul—men who have also much of the prophet and poet in their natures. He showed how the story of "Faust" is rooted in the consciousness of man; how the question which it raises stands like a vast interrogation mark, a symbol of thirst and search, at the first and at the last gate through which man's experience takes him.

Goethe's answer, in so far as he made one in "Faust", is not the answer all men would make. His gospel of striving, his romantic glorification of experience for its own sake, his implication that desire is an end rather than a means, a veritable good in itself—these would not content another kind of man who sees more good in reason than Goethe did. This other man might come to one of two conclusions, each of them different from Goethe's. He might discover an authority—in God, perhaps, or in reason itself—under which the mind, as Goethe's never did, could cease to be restless. Or he might, as Goethe never did, assert that the intellect has after all no hold upon phenomena, and certainly no correspondence with them; they move in their characteristic confusion for ever and ever, it moves in its characteristic clarity through a like eternity; and not at any point will the two things meet; there can be no ideas, in other words, about experience; one theory of life will be as good as any other, and all will be equally irrelevant. So might another man than Goethe speak, and for all I know he might be right. I am not interested in the question of rightness, however, or at any rate of Goethe's rightness. It is much more to the point, since he was a poet, to see how well he said what he had to say. And as to that there can be no disagreement. If with the majority of modern men, and as their spokesman, he chose to consider experience directly, and to conquer its confusion by accepting it, by mounting it and riding on its back, then there is much to say of his influence: he led the way. Yet even if he had led no procession, even if he had written and thought alone, he would have had to be called perfect in the thing he did. Wrestling with the problem of nature as centuries of skepticism had left it—the only problem of man, and a problem which man must solve, apparently, with no help from any god—he solved it for his purposes completely. Or rather he stated it for our purposes completely. We may ignore the problem in various ways. We may simply dismiss it as difficult and uninteresting, or we may escape from it into some kind of fantastic orthodoxy that momentarily comforts us. If we face it, however, we shall find ourselves facing Goethe too. He is there to stay, directly in the centre —poet, wise man, and director of the play.

A NOTE ON
THE ILLUSTRATIONS

ECKERMANN said to Goethe himself that the illustrations made by Delacroix contribute much to a better understanding of "Faust." "There is no question as to that," wrote Goethe in reply, "for the more perfect imagination of such an artist forces us to think the situations as well as he has thought them himself. I must now admit that M. Delacroix has surpassed my own conception in certain scenes!"

The Delacroix lithographs were first published by Motte in Paris in 1828, in a very large folio edition. From a portfolio of proofs of the lithographs in their very rare *first state*, they have now been reproduced, and for practical purposes in reduction, through the collotype process by Arthur Jaffé.

DEDICATION

Once more ye come, ye wavering forms that passed
In earlier days before my troubled sight.
Shall I endeavour now to hold ye fast?
In this illusion do I still delight?
Out of a misty, shadowy domain
Ye crowd about me! Good! Then take full sway,
For as in youth my heart is stirred again
By magic breath which round you seems to play.

A vision of happier days ye now unveil,
And wraiths of friends once dear to me arise;
As in an ancient, half-forgotten tale,
First love and friendship pass before my eyes.
Through plaintive echoes sorrow is revived,
Life's labyrinthine path again I see;
Friends are recalled who were by fate deprived
Of happy years, and so were lost to me.

They do not hear the songs which follow still,
Those souls to whom I gave my earliest song;
Forever scattered is the friendly throng,
And ah! That first response is mute and chill!
By many unknown to me my voice is heard,
Whose very praise intimidates my heart;
And they whom once my song so deeply stirred,
If they still live, are scattered far apart.

Unwonted yearning stirs me with desire
For that untroubled realm whence spirits rise;
My faltering song, faint as the Aeolian lyre,
Quavers unsteadily, then faintly dies.
A shudder seizes me! Tears follow tears,
My austere heart grows tender, and I feel
What I possess far, far away appears,
And only what has vanished now seems real.

THE PROLOGUE IN
THE THEATRE

MANAGER   DRAMATIC POET   COMIC PERSON

MANAGER You two who often stood by me
In days of trouble and of need,
Tell me, whether in Germany
Our undertaking will succeed?
I want to please the crowd we get,
Because it lives and lets us live; each seat
Is ready, our booth is up, the stage is set,
And everyone is waiting for a treat.
Already in their places with eyebrows raised,
They sit composed and want to be amazed.
The public I know how to interest,
But into such a fix I've ne'er been led;
It's true they're not accustomed to the best,
Yet what a frightful lot they've read!
How shall we ever make things fresh and new,
Contain a meaning, yet be pleasing too?
Frankly, I delight to watch the throng,
As towards our booth it streams along;
Then with a powerful repeated flow,
Through narrow, favored gates the people go;
By daylight, ere the hour of four,
Around the ticket box they start a row;
As folk in famine storm the baker's door,
They almost break their necks for tickets now.
The poet's miracle alone can sway
Such various minds; O friend, do this to-day!

POET   O speak not of that motley throng!
        One glance compels my spirit into flight!
        Veil from me the crowd which whirls along
        And sucks us in the vortex 'gainst our will!
        No! lead me to a nook divinely still,
        Wherein the poet alone finds pure delight,
        Where love and friendship with divine control
        Create and train the gifts of heart and soul.
        What from our deepest being seemed to course,
        What bashful lips tried shyly to express,
        Sometimes with failure, sometimes with success,
        Is swallowed by a violent moment's force.
        Oft when slowly ripened many a year,
        Will the perfected form appear.
        What glitters lives an instant, then is gone;
        The real for all posterity lives on.

COMIC PERSON   Posterity? That word offends my ears!
        Suppose I talked of future years,
        Who would amuse the world to-day?
        They want and ought to have their fun;
        A lad of spirit in your play
        Has value too when all is said and done.
        The public's moods will never irritate
        The man who gives himself with charm and ease;
        He'll long for larger crowds to animate,
        To rouse and sway as he may please.
        Pluck up and show what you can do!
        Bring Phantasy with her attendants here!
        Let Feeling, Passion, Reason, Sense appear—
        But mark you! let us have some Nonsense too!

MANAGER   Mind you, let Action also have its share!
        They come to see, but they prefer to stare.
        If you will only spin off all you can,
        Set wondering crowds a-gaping with delight,
        Virtually the goal will be in sight,

And you will be a popular man.
The masses by mass alone an author swings,
Each one eventually selects his fare;
He who brings much, something to many brings,
And each one leaves contented with his share.
If giving a piece, give it in pieces now!
Such hash I'm sure you can prepare;
Easy to give, it's easily invented;
Why bother with a whole, when what's presented,
The public will pick to pieces anyhow!

POET How base such hack-work is! Do you not feel
It is unworthy of an artist's soul?
You've made a virtue which you would extol
Out of the stuff and nonsense in which you deal!

MANAGER Rebukes of that kind don't offend!
A serious worker must depend
Upon the tools which he considers good.
Remember, you're required to split soft wood!
Just look about—whom are you writing for?
While this one comes as bored as bored can be,
Another comes who dined too heavily.
And frankly what I most abhor,
Some from reading their papers run to me.
They rush here, heedless, as to a masquerade,
Spurred on by curiosity alone;
The ladies play their parts yet are not paid,
Showing off in all the finery they own.
What do you dream of in your poet's sphere?
How does a crowded house affect your mood?
Study your patrons well, draw near,
Half are indifferent, half are rude!
One wants a game of cards after the play,
One in the arms of a wench, a wanton night,
So why, poor fools, annoy and pray
The Muses for an end so trite!

I tell you, give them more—more than they ever ask:
Then from your goal you cannot go far wrong;
Attempt to mystify the throng,
To satisfy them is too hard a task.
What's come over you—elation or disgust?

POET   Go, seek another slave! O must
The poet take the highest gift we know,
The human gift which Nature did bestow,
And squander it upon a wanton show?
How does he stir all hearts and how control
The elements? Is it not by harmony of soul,
He draws the world into his heart again?
When round the distaff Nature winds
With unconcern the thread of life,
And when discordant beings of all kinds,
Twisted together, clash in cruel strife,
Infusing life, who makes the separation
By which they fall in order rhythmically?
Who summons to universal consecration
The Individual, creating harmony?
Who makes the tempest rage with passionate wrath?
Who makes you feel the glowing sunset hours?
Who scatters all the fairest, budding flowers
Of spring over the Belovèd's path?
Who twines the evergreens with simple rites,
Merit in every field to glorify?
Who makes Olympus safe, the gods unites?
The power of Man which poets personify!

COMIC PERSON   Then use the powers by which you're swayed
To carry on the poet trade
Much as you would some love-affair!
By chance you meet—are stirred—you linger there,
And little by little you are involved;
Joy waxes—then it is dissolved;
Rapture comes first, but swiftly looms—despair!

Before you know it, you've a romance there!
Let's also try to give a play like this;
Probe the depths of life, its pain, its bliss.
Each lives it, although understood by few,
It's full of interest wherever grasped by you.
With varicolored pictures, not too clear,
Much error and a spark of truth,
The best drink will be brewed to cheer
And edify the world. Then youth
In all its fairest flower, will arrive,
And as a revelation hail your play;
While sentimental natures will derive
Their melancholy food from what you say.
First at this and then at that they'll start,
As each perceives what's buried in his heart.
They come prepared to laugh or cry with ease,
Pathos they applaud, illusion they adore;
Who deems himself complete is hard to please,
A maturing soul is grateful evermore.

POET Then give me back those years long past
When I could still mature and grow,
And when a spring of song welled fast
Out of my heart with ceaseless flow!
When all the world was veiled in mist,
When every bud a miracle concealed,
And when I gathered myriad flowers
Crowding the valley and the field.
Though naught was mine, I had enough in youth,
A joy in illusion, a longing for the Truth.
Give back the sweep of surging impulse, re-create
That happiness so steeped in pain,
The power of love, the strength of hate—
O give me back my youth again!

COMIC PERSON Youth, my friend, you'll need in any case,
When enemies in combat press;

Or when a lovely girl whom you caress,
Clings to you in close embrace.
Or when the victor's wreath from a distant site
Lures you to a goal unwon,
Or, after a frenzied dance and wanton fun,
Feasting and drinking you pass the night.
But, to strike the well-known chords with strength,
With courage and with animation,
While to a self-appointed goal at length
You ramble with pleasant deviation,
That, aged sirs, should be your task to-day,
And we esteem you for it none the less;
Age does not make us childish, as people say,
But finds us children still—I must confess!

MANAGER Sufficient words have been exchanged;
Come, let us have action move apace!
While compliments are being arranged,
Something useful could take place.
Why all this talk of inspiration?
It never comes to people who delay!
If you think yourself a poet—no hesitation,
Command the Muse of Poetry to obey!
You know quite well what we require!
Let's sip strong drink with spark and fire.
Brew it at once, it's time it was begun;
What's not done now, to-morrow won't be done.
Let not one single day slip past;
Let resolution then be bold,
Clasping occasion by the forelock fast;
And since it must, and won't let go its hold,
It labors staunchly to the last.
Upon our German stage you know
Each tries out what he wants to see;
So don't be stingy putting on your show,
With either props or scenery.
Use both the heavenly lights, the great and small,

Scatter the stars with a lavish hand;
Water, fire, rocky wall,
Birds and beasts, all are at your command.
Thus in our narrow booth to-day,
Creation's ample scope display,
And wander swiftly, yet observing well,
From Heaven through the world to Hell.

THE PROLOGUE IN HEAVEN

THE ALMIGHTY   THE HEAVENLY HOSTS

Afterwards MEPHISTOPHELES

THE THREE ARCHANGELS step forward

RAPHAEL The sun is chanting his ancient song
In contest with the brother spheres,
Rolling with thunder steps along,
Down the predestined course of years.
His presence gives the angels might,
Though fathom it none ever may;
And Thy sublime works still are bright
With splendor of Creation's day.

GABRIEL While swift and ever swifter swings
The world with glory into sight,
And heavenly light on golden wings
Yields to the shuddering depths of night;
In foaming waves the sea is flung
Against the rocks with swirling force;
Then rock and sea are pulled and swung
In the spheres' eternal course.

MICHAEL While storms an angry struggle wage
From sea to land, from land to sea,
Forging a mightly chain in rage
Of ever-flowing energy.
Beyond lies blazing desolation,
Where crashing thunder flames its way;
Thy heralds, though, in adoration
Revere Thy gently changing day.

MEPHISTOPHELES: I like to meet the Chief from time to time;
On pleasant terms I take good care to stay.

THE THREE TOGETHER

> This vision gives the angels might,
> Though fathom it none ever may,
> And all Thy lofty works are bright,
> With splendor of Creation's day.

MEPHISTOPHELES

> Since you, O Lord, once more are drawing near
> To question us how matters seem to be,
> Since once it pleased you seeing me—well, here
> Amongst these lackeys—gaze on me!
> Excuse me, but I can't be eloquent,
> Not even though I'm scorned by all your staff;
> My pathos would provoke your merriment,
> Had you not quite forgotten how to laugh.
> Of suns and worlds I've not one word to say:
> How men torment themselves is all I see!
> That little earth-god stays the same eternally,
> And is as odd as on Creation's day.
> He would be better off, in life at least,
> Had you withheld the spark of celestial light;
> He calls it reason, using it as right
> To be more animal than any beast.
> Saving your gracious presence, he seems to be
> Like a lanky grasshopper which ceaselessly
> Keeps flying about, and flying springs,
> Then back in the grass the same old ditty sings.
> Were he but satisfied as in the grass he lies!
> But no, he digs his nose in all the dirt he spies.

THE ALMIGHTY

> Have you nothing more to say?
> Must you endlessly complain?
> Is nothing ever right on earth?

MEPHISTOPHELES

> No, Lord, life is as rotten as before!
> I pity men, in misery from birth;
> I even hate to plague them any more.

THE ALMIGHTY Do you know Faust?

MEPHISTOPHELES   The Doctor?

THE ALMIGHTY   My servant!

MEPHISTOPHELES Indeed he serves you in a curious fashion!
No earthly food and drink allays his passion;
An inner tumult drives him far,
Yet of his frenzy he's but half aware.
From heaven he demands the fairest star,
From earth all joys supremely rare,
Yet neither what is near nor what is far
Can ease his restless breast, his buried care.

THE ALMIGHTY Although he serves me now bewilderedly,
I soon will lead him where the light is clear.
Does not the gardener know, when fresh green tips the
    tree,
That flower and fruit will deck the coming year!

MEPHISTOPHELES What do you wager? You will lose that man
If you permit me then to lead
Him subtly into the path I plan.

THE ALMIGHTY As long as he remains on earth—agreed!
Nothing is forbidden you contrive;
Man errs so long as he will strive.

MEPHISTOPHELES Thank you! Frankly, for the dead
I never hankered much; instead
I'd rather have a cheek quite plump and red.
I'm out if ever a corpse comes to my house;
I act just as a cat does with a mouse!

THE ALMIGHTY So be it, it is your affair!
Divert this spirit from its primal source,
And, if you can attract him, drag him where
You go upon your downward course;
Then stand ashamed, forced to admit, contrite.

That Man, through all his obscure, striving urge,
Is ever conscious of the path to right.

MEPHISTOPHELES Agreed! And I will make short work of it!
Of my wager I've no fear.
But if I should succeed, will you permit
That, swelling with triumph, I then venture here?
Dust shall he eat, and that with gusto too,
As my relative the snake was wont to do.

THE ALMIGHTY Here too, you have a free hand openly;
I never have abhorred your sort and kind.
Of all denying spirits known to me,
Least does the waggish knave offend my mind.
Too quickly stilled is man's activity,
Too soon he longs for unconditioned rest;
Hence I bestowed this comrade willingly,
Who goads, and as a devil, creates best.
But ye, God's own true Sons, enjoy and bless
Life and its abundant loveliness.
May the creative and eternal might
Clasp you in bonds which lofty love has wrought;
May that which fluctuates in drifting light
Be fortified by permanence of thought.
                    The Heavens close; the Archangels separate

MEPHISTOPHELES *alone*

I like to meet the Chief from time to time;
On pleasant terms I take good care to stay.
How kind of such a dignitary to chat
Even with the Devil, in this human way!

I

NIGHT

A narrow high-vaulted Gothic room; FAUST sits
restlessly in his chair at his desk

FAUST   I've studied all Philosophy,
Medicine, Jurisprudence too,
Also, to my grief, Theology,
With fervent efforts through and through;
Yet here I stand, poor fool! what's more
Not one whit wiser than before!
I'm Master, Doctor, and I've found
For ten long years, that as I chose
I've led my students by the nose,
First up, then down, then all around,
To see that nothing can be known!
This cuts me to the quick, I'll own!
I'm cleverer than all that tribe—
Doctor, Lawyer, Parson, Scribe;
All doubts and scruples I dispel,
I have no fear of devil or hell,
Wherefore I'm shorn of joy as well.
I don't think much of what I know,
I don't imagine I could show
How men could ever mend their ways,
Or help them on to better days.

Not even property or gold,
Or worldly honors do I hold!
No dog would stand this any more!
Therefore I've turned to magic lore,
So that, through supernatural force,
I'll trace many a secret to its source
And need no longer sweat and grieve
To teach what I do not believe;
So I'll discern what forces bind
The world together, and I'll find
What forces move the stirring seed,
And from spinning empty words be freed!

O glowing moon, didst thou but shine
A last time on this pain of mine!
Behind this desk how oft have I
At midnight seen thee rising high!
O'er books and papers when I'd bend,
Thou didst appear, O mournful friend!
Ah, could I on some mountain height
Roam in thy softly tender light,
Over the fields at twilight trail,
Drifting with spirits of hill and dale;
Then freed from knowledge and its pain,
Bathed in thy dew my health I'd gain.

Ah, am I still imprisoned here, alone?
Damnable dungeon walls of stone,
Where even the light of heaven waves
Drearily through the painted panes!
Hemmed in by a toppling, dusty mound
Of worm-eaten volumes without end
Which up to the vaulted arch extend,
With smoke-stained manuscripts around?
With glasses and boxes, crammed and packed,
With instruments, together hurled,
Ancestral stuff, heaped up and stacked—
That is your world! That's called a world!

Do you then wonder why your heart
Is cramped within your breast by dread,
Why an unexplainable pain and smart
Chokes feelings once flowing free?—Instead
Of Nature's genial, living sphere
Into which Man by God was thrust,
These skeletons surround you here
Of beasts and men, in mold and dust!

Be off! Away! To broad, free lands!
This volume wherein mysteries hide,
From Nostradamus' very hands,
Is not this book sufficient guide?
Then the course of stars you'll learn,
And Nature, teaching you, will fill
Your soul with power; then you'll discern
How spirits to spirits speak at will!
All this dry pondering is in vain
The holy symbols to explain.
Ye hover, spirits, near me . . . near!
Answer me, if you can hear!

> He opens the book and gazes upon the sign
> of the Macrocosm

Ha! at this one burning glance what ecstasy
Courses through my senses once again!
I feel a youthful holy joy of life,
Quivering through every nerve and vein!
Was it a god who wrote this sign which stills
My inner tumult, fills
My troubled heart with joy,
And with mysterious force reveals
The power of Nature which about me steals?
Am I a God? My spirit grows so clear!
I gaze on this fine script, and here
Nature at work, bared to my soul, I feel!
At last I understand the sage who said,
"The World of Spirits is not barred to thee!

Thy mind is sealed! Thy heart is dead!
Up, student! Bathe unweariedly
Thy earthly breast in morning-red."

> He contemplates the sign

How in the universal all things blend,
And in each other live and grow!
How heavenly forces soar aloft, descend,
Then in and out of golden flagons flow,
While fragrant blessings lightly wing
From heaven through the earth and bring
Harmonies which through the Whole now ring!

What a pageant! But after all—only a show!
Where shall I grasp thee, illimitable Nature?
Ye breasts, from which all life doth flow,
To which my withered soul must strive,
Earth and heavens ye sustain,
Ye flow, ye nourish—yet must I long in vain?

> He turns over the pages of the book impatiently and
> perceives the sign of the Earth-Spirit

How differently I am affected by this sign!
Thou, Spirit of Earth, art nearer me!
Already I feel suffused as if with wine.
I feel new strength to face the world again,
To endure all earthly joy, all earthly pain,
To battle through all storms with might and main,
From crashing shipwreck rise and still attain!
Clouds are gathering . . .
The moon conceals her light . . .
The lamp is flickering low!
Mists rise! Red flashes, sparkling bright,
Play about my head! A chilling breath
Creeps downwards from the vaulted roof
Gripping me fast!
I feel thee hovering near, O Spirit oft invoked!
Reveal thyself at last!

Ah, how my beating heart is choked!
With new emotions
My senses are rife!
I feel that all my heart goes out to thee!
Thou must! thou must! although it cost my life!

> He seizes the book and pronounces mysteriously the
> invocation of the Earth-Spirit. A reddish flame bursts
> forth and the Spirit appears in the flame

SPIRIT Who calls?

FAUST *turning away*
    O terrifying face!

SPIRIT With compelling power hast thou drawn me here,
And thou has long drawn sustenance from my sphere,
Yet now—

FAUST O! I cannot endure thee!

SPIRIT Breathlessly didst thou beg to look on me,
To hear my voice, my countenance to see,
To the powerful yearning of thy soul I bow.
Here, then, am I!—What pitiable horror now
Grips thee, superman! Where are the soul's outcries—
The self which from its depths a world created,
Tended and cherished it, then, by ecstasy dilated,
To us, the Spirits, sought to rise!
Where art thou, Faust, whose voice rang in my ears,
Who aspired to me with overwhelming might?
Art thou he, who at my first breath appears
To be a cringing, terror-stricken worm,
Trembling to the marrow in his fright?

FAUST Creature of flame, why should I flinch before thee?
Yes, it is Faust, thy equal, I am he!

SPIRIT In the tides of life, in action's storm,

Rising, sinking, I flow
To and fro!
Birth and death are to me
An eternal sea,
A changing and weaving,
Life glowing and seething;
Thus toiling at the humming loom of time and fate,
The living robe of the Godhead I create.

FAUST Thou who dost encompass the wide world,
Creative Spirit, how similar we are!

SPIRIT Thou resemblest the Spirit thou canst understand
Not me!

Disappears

FAUST *overwhelmed*

Not thee?
Whom then?
I, image of the Godhead,
Not even like thee?

A knock

Good grief, my famulus—to-night!
That is the end to my rare joy!
Why must that shriveled grind destroy
My glorious vision at its height!

*Enter Wagner in a dressing-gown and a nightcap, a
lamp in his hand. Faust turns to him reluctantly*

WAGNER I heard you, pardon me, declaiming a part;
One of the Grecian tragedies no doubt?
I'd like to gain more practice in this art,
As nowadays it helps one out.
I've often heard men boasting that a preacher
Does well to take an actor for his teacher!

FAUST Yes, if the preacher is inclined
To be an actor, as you sometimes find.

WAGNER Immured within a study, how can men
        Who scarcely ever see the world, and then
        Only from afar as through a telescope,
        To guide it by persuasion ever hope?

FAUST   Unless you feel—pursuit will be in vain.
        Unless this feeling surges from your soul
        With primal force of pleasure, to control
        Your listeners' hearts—if this you cannot gain—
        Just sit forever! Patch and glue each bit,
        From someone else's feast concoct a stew,
        Puffing the wretched flame you've lit
        Out of your puny ash-heap too!
        Making apes and children gape and start
        Is all very fine—if that is what you seek!
        But you will never link a heart to heart,
        Unless out of your heart you freely speak.

WAGNER Elocution makes the orator though;
        I feel that I have very far to go.

FAUST   Strive for an honorable success!
        Be no tinkling fool in your address!
        Common sense and truth don't need
        Either art or much display;
        Why hunt high-sounding words indeed,
        If you have something true to say?
        Those speeches, filled with tinsel words, which try
        To fool humanity with childish prattle,
        Are lifeless as the misty winds which sigh,
        And through the withered leaves in autumn rattle!

WAGNER Ah God! How long is Art,
        While Life is brief!
        Critical efforts often leave my heart
        And mind depressed with grief.
        How difficult to gain the means whereby
        A man may rise and reach the source!

And ere he covers half the given course,
Alas, poor devil! he must die.

FAUST   Is parchment then the sacred spring that pours
A draught which evermore will slake your thirst?
No, no, refreshment never will be yours,
Unless deep from your soul it gushes first!

WAGNER   Pardon! but it is a treat to cast
Ourselves into the spirit of the past,
To see what sages formerly expressed,
Then to what noble heights we have progressed!

FAUST   O yes! Unto the stars on high!
The ages of the past, my friend,
Are to us a book of seven seals; what you suspected
To be the spirit of the times, proves in the end
To be your spirit—nothing more—
In which the ages are reflected.
This we frequently deplore,
And men but glance at it, then run away.
'Tis but an attic, a rubbish nest,
At most a mere political display,
Pragmatic maxims, phrases in a way
Which suit the mouths of puppets best!

WAGNER   But then the world—man's heart—his soul,
If each could know a portion of the whole!

FAUST   Yes, what one calls knowing! Who dares claim
To give the child its rightful name?
The few who knew somewhat, who did not shield
Their brimming hearts, but foolishly revealed
Their thoughts and feelings to the mob—they always
     died
At the stake, or else were crucified.
But it is dead of night! Excuse me, friend,
Our conversation now must end.

WAGNER   I should have shared your vigil with delight,
           And carried on our learned talk all night.
           I'll bring to-morrow, since it's Easter Day,
           These and other questions if I may
           I've studied zealously, and though
           I know so much—still, all I'd like to know.

                Exit

FAUST   *alone*

           How hope does not abandon such a brain,
           To shallow stuff forevermore glued fast!
           He digs with greedy hands for hidden gain,
           Delighted if he finds a worm at last!

           How dare the voice of such a man resound,
           Where in profusion spirits hovered around!
           But ah, this time my deepest thanks you've won,
           Earth's most miserable son!
           You snatched me from the dark despondency
           Which threatened to destroy my mind before;
           The vision was so stupendous, that I see
           I am a dwarf, a dwarf and nothing more!

           I, God's image, who already thought
           To near the mirror of eternal Truth, who sought
           To revel in clarity and heavenly light,
           Freed from mortal plight—
           I, more than Cherub, whose unbridled force
           Presumed to flow through Nature's veins,
           And, like the gods creating, sought their planes,
           How I am punished! From my lofty course
           A word of thunder swept me back aghast.

           I do not dare compare myself to thee!
           I had the power to draw thee close to me,
           Yet not the force by which to hold thee fast.
           When in that holy moment I seemed to be
           So little, yet so very great,

Thou didst thrust me cruelly
Back into uncertainties of human fate.
Whose teaching shall I heed? What shall I shun?
Shall I obey each inner urge?
Alas! our deeds, as well as sorrows, one by one
Clog the current of our life's deep surge.
To lofty glories which our soul receives,
Strange and stranger substance always cleaves;
When in the good of this world we can share,
We call the better a delusion and a snare;
Whilst noble feelings given us by life
Congeal in a universe of restless strife.

If Phantasy on daring wings once in the past,
Swelled by hope, sailed into infinite space;
Yet now she is satisfied with a little place,
Since joy after joy in the whirlpool of time is cast.
Care nestles in the depths of every heart,
There causing many a secret sorrow,
Restlessly rocking, driving joy and peace apart,
Disguised with changing masks each morrow,
It seems to be house or land, or child or wife,
Or fire, water, poison, steel;
Though nothing happens, dread you always feel,
What you never lose, you mourn throughout your life.

Not like the gods! Too conscious of this am I!
I am like the worm which burrows through the dust
And, seeking there its sustenance, is crushed
And buried by a passer-by!

Is it not dust, wherewith these towering walls
With hundred shelves imprison me,
This countless rubbish which has endlessly
Confined me to these mouldy halls?
Here shall I satisfy my need?
What though in a thousand volumes I should read
That human beings suffered everywhere,

That by mere chance was one man happy here and
    there?
Why grin, you hollow skull, except to say
That once your brain, perplexed like mine,
Yearning for Truth, pursued the light of day,
Then in the dusk went wretchedly astray?
Ye instruments, ye jeer at me, I feel,
Cog and circle, cylinder and wheel!
I stood at the door, ye should have been the key;
Though fashioned well, ye raised no latch for me.
Unfathomable by light of day,
Nature will permit no one to steal
Her veil; what to the spirit she will not reveal,
With lever and screw you cannot wrest away.
Old instruments, though never used by me,
Because ye served my father ye remain;
Old scrolls, by taint of smoke ye have been stained,
Since first this desk-lamp smouldered drearily.
Wiser to have squandered the little I possessed,
Than to sit and sweat here by that little oppressed.
All that your ancestors bequeathed to you,
To make it really yours, earn it anew.
That which is useless is a burden sore;
What each moment creates it uses—nothing more.

Yet why is my glance attracted to that place?
Is that small phial a magnet for my sight?
Why does the room seem suddenly so bright
As if moonbeams drifted through dark woodland space?

O rare and precious phial, hail to thee,
Which now I take down reverently;
In thee I honor both man's wit and art.
O epitome of sleeping essence—thou
Extract of subtle, deadly powers—impart
Thy favor to thy master now!
I look upon thee—pain grows less to me!

I grasp thee—conflicts wane immediately!
Slowly the tides of my spirit ebb more and more,
Towards high seas I am being drawn from sight;
Before me a mirrored ocean sparkles bright,
A new day lures me to a newer shore!

Toward me, floating on airy wing,
A fiery chariot drifts! Ah, I prepare
To pierce new coursings of the air,
Through spheres of purer activity to swing!
This higher life, this godlike bliss,
Do you, but now a worm, deserve all this?
Only be resolute and boldly turn
Your back upon this sunny world! Yes, learn
To fling those portals wide
From which men gladly turn aside!
Lo! the hour has come to prove by deed
That manhood to the Godhead will not cede,
Not, facing the gloomy cavern, flinch and sway,
Where phantasies, self-tortured dwell;
But ever striving to that passageway
About whose narrow mouth flames all of hell,
Calmly to take this step, though none the less
The price may be—the plunge into nothingness!

O clearest crystal cup, come from thy place,
Forth from thy ancient leather case,
Thou whom I have not thought of many a year!
Sparkling at ancestral feasts thou didst appear,
Enlivening in turn each solemn guest
As thou wert passed from hand to hand; it was a test
For every drinker then in rhyme to tell
The meaning of the pictures graven well,
Then at one draught to drain thee to the end.
This brings back youthful memories to my heart.
I shall not pass thee now to any friend,
Nor shall I test my wit upon thine art.

Here is a swiftly intoxicating juice
Whose brownish fluid fills thy hollow bowl,
Which I prepare and which I choose,
Grant that this last drink be, with all my soul,
A festal salutation to the dawn!

He puts the goblet to his lips

CHURCH BELLS AND CHOIR

CHORUS OF THE ANGELS

Christ is arisen!
Joy be to those mortals
Whom cringing, inherited sin and corruption
Held in a prison
Of death and destruction!

FAUST   What vibrant sounds, what voices clear and fair
Withdraw the goblet from my lips with power?
Ye sonorous bells, already do ye declare
Easter with its first and sacred hour?
Ye choirs, sing ye that consoling chant
Which rang one night of death from angels' lips
In certainty of a newer covenant?

CHORUS OF THE WOMEN

With balm and the sweet-smelling
Spices we strew,
We tended and laid him down,
We who were true;
Now binding, now winding
Pure linen around;
Yet ah! when we seek him,
Christ is not found.

CHORUS OF THE ANGELS

Christ is ascended!
May the Belovèd be blest
Whose afflicting yet strengthening,
Chastening test
And trial is ended.

FAUST: Why grin, you hollow skull?

FAUST Why seek me, prostrate in this dusty cell,
Ye heavenly tones, so powerful yet mild?
Ring out beyond where gentle beings dwell!
Though I lack belief, I hear the tidings well;
The miracle is faith's most treasured child.
I dare not strive towards those distant spheres
From which these blessed tidings rain;
These tones, familiar since my childhood years,
Are calling me to life again.
Long, long ago a kiss of heavenly love
Descended on me during Sabbath rest;
Then bells with mystic meaning chimed above,
Prayer was a fervent joy which filled my breast.
A sweet yet unexplainable yearning
Drove me through the forest and the field,
And while my eyes with tears were burning
I felt in me another world revealed.
Of merry youthful play these anthems sing,
Of freedom and the happiness of spring;
With childish feeling memory thrusts me far
From this last solemn step of pain.
Ring on, ring on, belovèd songs of heaven!
My tears are flowing, earth claims me once again!

CHORUS OF THE DISCIPLES

Has He, the buried One,
Living, exalted Son,
Risen already
To glory on high?
In desire of Becoming
To creative joy is He nigh?
On the breast of earth, suffering,
Ah, here we must lie!
Yearning, He left us,
His followers, below;
Ah, Master, we cry for
The bliss Thou dost know!

CHORUS OF THE ANGELS

Christ has transcended
The womb of Corruption!
Let the bonds of destruction
Be joyfully rended!
To those serving through deeds,
Spreading love by their teaching,
Sustaining men in their needs,
Bearing tidings and preaching,
He not only is near,
He is verily here!

II

BEFORE THE CITY GATE

Pedestrians of all sorts come forth

SEVERAL APPRENTICES
    Why are you going up that way?

SEVERAL OTHERS We're going to the Hunters' Lodge on the hill.

FIRST GROUP We would rather stroll to the Mill.

ONE OF THE APPRENTICES
    Take my advice, go to the River Inn to-day!

A SECOND ONE The road up there is none of the best.

ONE OF THE SECOND GROUP
    And you?

A THIRD ONE   I'll follow with the rest.

A FOURTH ONE Come to Burgdorf! There you're bound to find
The prettiest girls, beer of the finest kind,
And first-class rough-and-tumble sport.

A FIFTH ONE You gay dog, are you itching still
For a third sound licking of that sort?
I won't go there, it makes me ill.

A SERVANT-GIRL No, I'm going back, and right away.

ANOTHER GIRL We're sure to find him by the poplar tree.

THE FIRST ONE Well, that's no such joy for me!
I know he'll hang round you all day,
And dance with you or else with none:
What's there for me in all your fun?

THE OTHER GIRL He will not be alone; he said,
"I am going to bring 'Curly-Head.' "

A STUDENT Hell! how those husky creatures step along!
Here, boy, let's join them! Come, make haste!
Biting tobacco, some beer good and strong,
And a servant-girl dressed up—h'm, that's my taste.

A CITIZEN'S DAUGHTER

Look at those handsome fellows, if you please!
Really it's a shame! Just see,
Though they could go in the best society,
They run after servant-girls like these!

A SECOND STUDENT *to the first*

Not so fast! There come two right behind,
Who are stylishly dressed! Why, what is more,
One is my little neighbor next door!
I've taken a fancy to her! You will find,
Although they walk primly, and act so sedate,
They won't mind if we pick them up—h'm, just you
    wait!

THE FIRST STUDENT

I hate to be embarrassed, it sickens me!
Hurry, lest these birds make a get-away!
The hand which plies the broom on Saturday
On Sunday fondles you more eagerly.

A CITIZEN No, I don't like him, the new Burgomaster!
Since he is in office his pride swells up faster
Each day! Really, what does he do for the town?
Conditions are steadily growing much worse;

We obey and obey till our life is a curse,
While taxes are more than we ever paid down.

A BEGGAR *singing*

Kind sirs, fair ladies, whom I see
With rosy cheeks and handsome dress,
Be good enough to look at me!
O look and lessen my distress!
O let me not strum on in vain!
Only the generous are gay.
Since all men celebrate this day,
May it be for me a harvest-gain!

ANOTHER CITIZEN On Sundays and holidays what I adore
Is to gossip of war and all of its scare,
Whilst far off in Turkey the foreign folk there
Continue to fight just as much as before.
One stands at the window, sipping one's glass,
Seeing the flagged vessels glide down the river;
When night comes, then one is contented to pass
Homewards, blessing peace and our era forever.

THIRD CITIZEN Yes, neighbor, I'm quite in agreement with you!
Let 'em all crack their skulls to the end of their days!
Let all go to pot, their scheming fall through!
But at home we will stick to our good old ways.

AN OLD WOMAN *To the Citizen's Daughter*

My, how dressed up! So young and so fair!
Who wouldn't lose his head over you!
Don't be stuck up! No harm's meant, I swear!
I know how to get you what you're wanting too!

THE CITIZEN'S DAUGHTER

Come Agatha! I am afraid to be seen
With an old witch like this—and in broad day;
Although she did show me on last Hallowe'en
My future sweetheart in a most lifelike way.

THE OTHER GIRL   She showed me mine too, in a clear crystal ball,
                 There he stood with some friends, a soldierly man;
                 I look all about me, I search all I can
                 But I've never yet met him in spite of it all.

THE SOLDIERS   Castles with battlement,
               Turret and tower,
               Maidens with arrogant
               Notions of power,
               I would obtain!
               Bold is the struggle,
               Mighty the gain!

               Let trumpets be sounding
               As we go by,
               Whether to pleasure,
               Or whether to die.
               O what a tempest!
               O what a life!
               Castles and women
               Must yield in such strife.
               Bold is the struggle,
               Mighty the gain,
               As all the soldiers
               Go marching amain.

                        Enter Faust and Wagner

FAUST   From icy bondage streams and brooks are freed
        By Spring's life-giving, lovely light;
        In the valleys hope and happiness swell the seed,
        While weak old Winter, creeping out of sight,
        Back to the rugged mountains must proceed.
        From there, still hastening his swift retreat,
        He scatters impotent showers of hail and sleet
        In furrows o'er the fields of dawning green.
        But the sun permits no glimpse of white be seen,
        Creative surging pulses everywhere.

Nature seeks more color and more grace,
And, as the meadow-lands of flowers are bare,
People in bright garments take their place.
Turn around, and from this height look down
Backwards on the little town.
See how the motley crowd with one accord
Surges from the hollow, gloomy gate!
Each suns himself with joy to celebrate
The resurrection of the Lord.
'Tis they are resurrected from their past!
From dingy rooms in shabby houses cast,
From bondage to their trade, by toil harassed,
From crowded street and narrow alleyway,
From oppressive roofs and gables gray,
From the Church's sacramental night,
All are guided to the light.
Look! how nimbly the crowds below
Scatter in the fields and gardens to and fro,
And how upon the river sway
Many little vessels gay,
Whilst, almost sinking with its load,
The last skiff pushes out of sight.
Even from the distant mountain road,
The colored raiment flashes bright.
Already we hear the noise of town, the cries,
Truly this is the people's paradise!
Here great and small shout out contentedly;
Here I am human—here human I can be!

WAGNER Doctor, to take a walk with you
Is an honor and profitable too;
But I should not care to wander here alone,
For I detest vulgarity!
This shrieking, bowling, all this fiddlery
Has a most obnoxious tone;
They act as if the Fiend possessed the throng,
And call this pleasure, call this song!

PEASANTS UNDER THE LINDEN TREE   *A song and a dance*

Heigho! for the dance the young shepherd was dressed,
With jacket and sash and a gay-colored vest,
With wreath and ribbons a-flying!
While under the linden each lass with her lad,
Under the linden they all danced like mad.
Hurrah! Tra-la-la!
Tra-la-la! Hurrah!
The fiddle and bow were crying.
He pushed and he shoved himself into the crowd,
Nudging a young girl who screamed aloud,
As his elbow kept a-plying;
The lively young creature turned round right away,
And said, "You're a stupid one, that's all I say!"
Hurrah! Tra-la-la!
Tra-la-la! Hurrah!
"You're a rude one, no denying!"
They flew round the circle with footsteps so light,
And petticoats a-flying!
They soon grew so red and they soon grew so warm
That they had to rest, panting, with arm linked in arm.
Hurrah! Tra-la-la!
Tra-la-la! Hurrah!
Elbow on hip a-lying.
"Now don't you make free quite so fast," said the maid;
"How many a girl has been sadly betrayed
With coaxing and with lying!"
Yet soon he had wheedled her off to one side,
While under the linden from far and from wide,
Hurrah! Tra-la-la!
Tra-la-la! Hurrah!
Came shrieks and the fiddle crying.

AN OLD PEASANT   Doctor, you are really very kind
To mix with us and not feel proud;
You, such a learned person, do not mind
Strolling midst this pushing crowd.

Accept our choicest jug to-day;
With cool sweet wine it has been filled.
I offer it, and wish to say,
Not only may your thirst be stilled,
But may your life-span ever gain
Days as many as the drops these cups contain.

FAUST I accept the jug and gladly too;
Good health to one and all of you.

The people form a circle about him

THE OLD PEASANT To tell the truth, it seems but right
That on a holiday you should appear,
You who in evil days gone by
Proved such a friend to all the people here.
How many a person is alive
Because of your father in the past
Snatched him out of raging fever,
When he checked the plague at last!
You entered every stricken house,
Though at that time a young man still;
Many a corpse was carried forth,
Yet you came through and were not ill,
Surviving many a trial in the end.
The friend was aided by the Heavenly Friend!

ALL THE PEASANTS

May good health bless the worthy man!
Long may he serve as best he can.

FAUST Bow down to Him whose teachings tell
Us how to serve, and who sends help as well.

He passes on with Wagner

WAGNER What feelings, O noble man, must rise in you
Before the veneration of this crowd!
O happy the man who gains such honors through

The gifts with which he is endowed!
The father shows you to his son,
People question, and crowd nearer one by one;
The fiddler stops, the dancers wait,
They form in rows, you pass in state,
While caps are waved and flung up high;
But little more and they would kneel
As if the Host were carried by.

FAUST   Only a few steps more, up to that stone!
Here, after our rambling, let us rest at last.
Here, lost in thought, I often sat alone,
Torturing myself with prayer and fast.
So rich in hope, so firm in faith was I,
With pleading hands, with tear and sigh,
The end of that dread plague I sought
From the Master of Heaven to extort.
The crowd's applause now sounds like scorn to me!
O could you read my inmost soul, you'd see
How little can the son or father claim
Such exaltation and such fame!
My father was a student of no great name,
Who brooded with curious labor day by day,
Yet honestly enough in his own way,
On Nature and her holy sphere.
In company with his adepts he withdrew
And, locked in his gloomy cubicle, would brew
And make opposing substances cohere
By means of endless formulas he knew.
A Lily and her suitor, a Lion red,
In a tepid bath were forced to wed;
Then both compelled by sudden burst of flame,
From bridal bath to bridal chamber came.
If in the glass the youthful Queen would glide
In varied colors, one could tell
This was the remedy! The patients died,
But no one questioned: "Who grew well?"

Delacroix imp¹ à Liberg

Ch. Motte imp¹ Editeur, à Paris.

Faust: O happy the man who hopefully aspires
Out of this sea of error to arise!

So we with hellish nostrums spread more ills
Throughout these valleys and these hills,
Causing far more damage than the pest!
Poison to thousands I myself did give;
They withered away, yet I must live
To see the shameless murderers blest.

WAGNER How can you yield to such despair!
Has not a good man done his share
By practicing with conscientious mind
The art entrusted to him by mankind?
If you revere your father as a youth
You'll learn from him with eager will;
If as a man, you further science, truth,
Your son may reach a goal far higher still.

FAUST O happy the man who hopefully aspires
Out of this sea of error to arise!
What man knows not, is just what he requires;
What man knows, he cannot use in any wise.
But let us not by gloomy spirits mar
This hour radiantly serene!
Behold! in the glow of sunset, from afar
The little houses shimmer, set in green.
The sun moves on and fades! The day is spent!
It hurries on to further fruitful birth.
Ah, that no pinions lift me from the earth
To follow close and closer its ascent!
Bathed in the eternal evening glow,
I would see the world beneath me, stilled;
The cliffs ablaze, the vales with quiet filled,
The Silberbach into golden streams would flow.
Not even the mountain gorge in wild display
Would then impede my godlike flight;
And soon the sea, each warmly sheltered bay,
Would lie before my wondering sight.
When it would seem the sun must sink at length,

A new urge fills me with new strength.
I hurry on to drink its eternal light,
Before me the day, behind me the night,
Heaven above, below the ocean swings;
A lovely dream while softly fades the sun!
Alas, but to our spiritual wings
No bodily wings are granted anyone!
Yet we are born with that desire
Which drives us up and onwards to aspire,
As o'er us, lost in space of azure sky,
Warbling its song, the lark must fly;
As o'er the steep pine-covered height,
The eagle spreads his wings in flight;
And o'er the marshes, o'er the sea,
The crane strives homewards hurriedly.

WAGNER   I too have often felt peculiar things,
Though not the impulse yet to which you yield;
One wearies soon of forest and of field,
And I shall never envy the bird his wings.
How different it is when mental pleasures lead
From book to book, from page to page we read.
Then winter evenings have a lovely charm,
And if by a sacred glow our limbs grow warm,
If then some precious parchment is unrolled,
All Heaven descends, its treasure to unfold!

FAUST   One impulse only are you conscious of,
O never learn to know the other state!
Alas! two souls within my breast abide,
And each from the other strives to separate.
The one, with love and healthy lust,
The world with clutching tentacles holds fast;
The other soars with power above this dust
Into the domain of our ancestral past.
O if there be spirits here,
Between the earth and heavens holding sway,

Descend now from the golden atmosphere,
Lead me to new and varied life away!
Yes, were a magic mantle only mine,
Away to foreign lands I'd lightly swing!
I would not change it for robes however fine,
Not even for the mantle of a king!

WAGNER Do not call upon that well-known swarm
Which permeates the vapory air;
From every corner they prepare
To injure men and do them harm.
From north with sharpened spirit-fangs they fly,
Pressing on you with arrow-pointed tongues;
From the east they move upon you, hard and dry,
Nourishing themselves upon your lungs.
Sent from the south, when the desert whirlwind drives,
They crown your head with glowing firebrands;
While from the west a host at first revives,
Then drowns you with the fields and pasture-lands.
They listen gladly, injure with fond intent,
Gladly obey, at cheating gladly try;
From Heaven feigning to be sent,
They lisp like angels when they lie.
But let us go! The world's becoming gray!
The air grows cool, mist falls to-day.
One learns to prize one's home at night.
Why do you stand and stare—what is the trouble?
What so attracts you in the failing light?

FAUST D'you see that black dog, rambling through corn and
stubble?

WAGNER Long ago! Not much to that as far as I can tell.

FAUST What do you take the beast to be? Observe it well!

WAGNER A poodle who, as dogs do, runs about
To trace his master's footsteps out.

FAUST   Watch how in wide concentric rings
         Near and nearer still to us he springs!
         If I'm not wrong, streams of fire fall
         Directly in his wake.

WAGNER   I see a plain black dog, that's all!
         The rest might be an optical mistake.

FAUST   He draws an airy, magic coil, it seems to me,
         For future bondage round our feet.

WAGNER   I see
         He jumps around, confused and filled with fear
         At seeing strangers, not his master here.

FAUST   The ring grows smaller, he is very near!

WAGNER   There—it's a dog, no phantom; that is clear!
         It crawls upon its belly, snarls in play,
         Wagging its tail in the usual doglike way.

FAUST   Come here to us! Come do!

WAGNER   The creature really is absurd!
         If you stand still, he'll wait for you,
         He'll leap upon you at a word;
         If something's lost, he'll fetch it quick,
         Or jump into the water for a stick.

FAUST   You're right; there's not a trace that I can call
         A spirit's; just sound training—that is all.

WAGNER   Even a sage would feel inclined
         To love a dog well-trained to mind.
         This pupil of the students is so smart
         That he deserves to have you take his part.

                   They pass through the gates of the city

Delacroix inv. et Lithog.   Lithog. de Ch. Motte à Paris.

WAGNER: There—it's a dog, no phantom; that is clear!
It crawls upon its belly, snarls in play,
Wagging its tail in the usual doglike way.

III

THE STUDY

FAUST entering with the poodle

FAUST Behind me, meadowland and field
Are by the depths of night concealed;
With awe and with foreboding might,
Our better self asserts its right.
Unruly desires sleep, and free
From passions' turbulence, and strain,
The love of man revives in me,

The love of God is stirred again.
Be quiet, poodle! Don't race about the floor!
Why do you sniff the threshold of the door?
Lie down behind the stove and, if you do,
I'll give my very best cushion to you.
Because you pleased us capering with zest
Upon the hilly thoroughfare,
I will accept you in my care,
Welcome, if you are a quiet guest!

Ah, when within our narrow cell,
The lamp has spread its friendly glow,
Then light into our breast will flow,
Into the heart which knows itself full well.
Reason begins once more to speak,
And hope begins to bloom again;
We yearn to seek life's flowing course—
Could we but reach its very source!

Stop snarling dog! That beastly noise is out of key
With sounds that sacredly
My very soul embrace!
Full well we know the human race
Will jeer at what it does not understand;
That men at loveliness and goodness scowl,
Qualities which they do not command.
Then will the dog, as they do, snarl and growl?

But ah! although my will is of the best,
Contentment flows no longer from my breast!
Why must the stream so soon be dried,
Leaving me to thirst once more?
I've felt this longing oft before,
Therefore I know this want can be supplied.
To prize the supernatural we learn,
For revelation's light we yearn,
Which nowhere shines in worthier light
Than here in our New Testament. . . . To-night
I feel compelled to open the basic text,
Then, with honest feeling, to render next
The sacred Original we teach
Into my own belovèd German speech.

He opens a volume and begins

"In the beginning was the Word!" Thus it doth say!
Here I'm balked! Who'll help me onward?
                                          . . . Why,
It's impossible to rate the Word so high,
I must translate it in another way
If by the Spirit truly inspired; I ought
To set down, "In the beginning was the Thought!"
Do not let your pen race on ahead,
Dwell upon this opening line instead.
That force creating, stirring—is it Thought indeed?
Then, "In the beginning was the Power," the text
    should read!

Yet even as I set down this command,
Something warns me that it cannot stand.
The Spirit aids me! Suddenly I grasp the fact,
And boldly write: "In the beginning was the Act!"

If we are to share this cell,
Dog, stop growling,
Stop that howling!
For I cannot stand, I fear,
Such a noisy comrade near.
One of us must say farewell
To this pleasant, quiet cell.
A truce to hospitality!
The door is open, you are free!
But whatever do I see!
Is this natural, can this be
A shadow? a reality?
How broad my dog becomes . . . how tall!
With power it rises, growing strong!
That's not a canine form at all!
What spectre have I brought along?
Almost a hippopotamus in size,
With dreadful jaws and blazing eyes.
Oh, indeed! Well, I know you!
For all of this half-hellish crew
The key of Solomon will do!

SPIRITS *in the corridor*

Someone is caught and fastened in!
Stay out, let no one follow him!
Like a fox in a snare
The Hell-Lynx quakes there.
But give heed, give heed!
Hover to and fro,
Above, below,
He will soon be freed!
If aid ye can search,
Leave him not in the lurch!

Many a good turn he's done
To everyone!

FAUST First, to face the mighty beast,
I need the spell of the Four at least!

Sparkle, Salamander!
Undine, meander!
Sylph, disappear!
Gnome, labor here!

He who cannot tell
These elements well,
Their power, their force
And properties, of course
He can never be lord
Of the spirit-horde.

Salamander, at thy name
Vanish into flame!
Rushing waters unite,
O Undine!
Glow like a meteor bright,
O Sylph!
Bring household aid and at thy call,
Incubus! Incubus!
Come forth—end it all!

These Four at least
Are not hid in that beast.
It lies quite still and grins at me!
I have not hurt him yet, I see!
Listen to me at length
Exorcise with more strength.

Fellow, art thou
A fugitive from Hell?
Behold the Sign

Which can compel
The dark hosts to incline.

With bristling hair it starts to swell!

Outcast Creature, take heed!
Canst thou not read
The sign of the Uncreated,
Whose name cannot be stated,
Who pervades the heavens from far and wide,
The Being wantonly crucified?

Behind the stove it's relegated,
Like an elephant inflated,
Into vapor swiftly stealing,
Filling up the room complete;
Do not rise up to the ceiling,
Down there, at your master's feet!
My threat is not an empty claim,
I'll scorch you with a holy flame!
Do not wait to know
The thrice dazzling glow!
Do not wait to know
My strongest art and strongest power!

> Mephistopheles, garbed as a travelling scholar, steps
> forward from behind the stove as the mist disappears

MEPHISTOPHELES   Why all this noise, sir? What can I do for you?

FAUST   So that was hidden in the brute! My word!
A travelling scholar! The thing is too absurd!

MEPHISTOPHELES   Good evening, learned sir! I declare
You certainly made me sweat for fair.

FAUST   What's your name?

MEPHISTOPHELES   A trifling question; what is more,
From one who spurns the Word entirely,

Who, disregarding externality,
Alone the depths of Being would explore.

FAUST With gentlemen like you one can discern
The nature if the name we learn;
Thus one knows well what it implies
To call you Destroyer, Liar, God of Flies;
Which, then, are you?

MEPHISTOPHELES   A part of that Might
Which ever willing Evil, ever makes for right.

FAUST Tell me what this riddle of yours implies!

MEPHISTOPHELES I am the Spirit that ever denies!
And justly so; for all that's born
Deserves to be destroyed in scorn.
Therefore 'twere best if nothing were created!
Destruction, sin, wickedness—plainly stated—
All which you as evil have classified,
That is my element, there I abide!

FAUST You call yourself a part, yet as a whole appear to me?

MEPHISTOPHELES I am telling you the simple facts,
Though man, that foolish cosmos, always acts
As if complete he thought himself to be.
I am part of that part which was the Absolute,
A part of that darkness which gave birth to light,
The arrogant light which would dispute
The ancient rank of Mother-Night,
To claim her space; and yet the struggle dies,
For light to matter cleaves with force.
From matter it flows, matter it beautifies,
Yet matter checks it on its course.
Therefore I hope it won't be long before,
With matter, it will perish evermore.

MEPHISTOPHELES: Why all this noise, sir? What can I do for you?

FAUST Now I grasp your worthy scheme!
Since universal ruin you cannot create,
You start upon a smaller theme.

MEPHISTOPHELES I've not accomplished much, I'll frankly state!
This power which against nothingness is hurled,
This something—this your clumsy world—
Though constantly I've tried to injure it
By earthquake, tempest, or volcanic flame,
Has not been really touched one bit!
In the end both land and sea remain the same.
As for the human and animal litter, that damnable stuff,
What I have managed there is little enough.
What endless numbers have I not wiped out!
Yet new blood ever circulates about.
So it goes on! It drives me frantic! Everywhere
From earth, from water, from the air,
In dry and wet, in warm and cold,
A million vital germs unfold;
Until, if I had not reserved the flame,
I should have nothing as my own to claim.

FAUST To the beneficent, creative force which you resist,
Eternally opposed, you thrust and strain
Your cold malignant devil's fist,
Spitefully clenched, yet clenched in vain!
You singular son of Chaos! I should say
A different task had best be sought.

MEPHISTOPHELES We'll give this matter further thought
And talk about it more another day.
Might I withdraw this time? Will you allow . . .

FAUST I don't see why you ask me that,
I've just begun to know you now.
Come whenever you want to have a chat;
Here's the window, and there the doors,
The chimney place is also yours.

MEPHISTOPHELES I must admit I cannot go!
A trifling hindrance makes me stay.
That wizard-foot upon your sill below—

FAUST So the pentagram is in your way?
Come, confess, you son of Hell,
How did you enter if you cannot leave?
A spirit like you, how could one deceive?

MEPHISTOPHELES Look carefully—it's not drawn well;
The outer angle, that one nearest me,
Is slightly open as you see.

FAUST That was a stroke of luck! So you,
You were my prisoner! Come, confess,
This episode is a great success!

MEPHISTOPHELES Leaping, in the dog saw nothing new,
But all is altered now; I know
That I, the devil, cannot go.

FAUST Why not slip through the window-frame?

MEPHISTOPHELES Devils and phantoms on this law agree:
Where they steal in, they must slip out again.
Slaves of the second law, of the first we're free.

FAUST So even Hell has its own laws! Why, then
Would it be possible to make
A binding compact with you gentlemen?

MEPHISTOPHELES We'll carry out the tasks we undertake;
You shall enjoy all that we promise you.
This cannot be swiftly brought about—
Let us discuss it next time, too;
To-night I beg you, let me out,
Spare me this time—let me go!

FAUST Only a moment more; do stay
And tell me some strange tale you know.

MEPHISTOPHELES Free me! I'll come back! You may
Then ask me what you please—I do not care.

FAUST You let yourself into the snare;
I did not set the trap to-night.
Who catches the devil should hold him tight;
A second time you will not catch him there.

MEPHISTOPHELES If you wish, I am prepared to stay
And keep you company awhile,
Provided that with arts I may beguile
And profitably pass your time away.

FAUST I'll watch you willingly indeed;
Let your arts be pleasing and proceed!

MEPHISTOPHELES My friend, in this one hour, freed,
Your senses will experience more
Than in all your humdrum years before.
Music the gentle spirits sing,
The lovely images they bring,
Are not mere magic phantasy.
First sense of smell will be invoked,
Next your palate be provoked,
Then feelings glow ecstatically!
We need not plan out any part,
We are together, come now—start!

THE SPIRITS *singing*

Vanish, ye gloomy
Arches on high!
Gaze on us,
Lovely and friendly
Blue sky!
O would the murky

Clouds disappear!
Tiny stars, sparkle,
Soft sunbeams,
Shine here.
Children of Heaven,
Spirits of Love,
Bowing and trembling,
Hover above.
Undying longing
Next we behold;
Soft flowing draperies
Wind and unfold,
Covering the bowers,
Covering the field,
Where for life, deep in reverie,
True lovers yield.
Bower on bower,
Tendrils entwine!
Clustering grapes
Gushing to wine.
Heaping in vats,
Leaping in streams,
Squeezed in the press,
Wine bubbles and steams,
And ripples o'er stones
Lovely and bright,
Then leaving behind
The glittering height,
Spreads into lakes
Of purest delight
To feed the green hills;
Where in swift flight,
Drinking pure bliss,
The feathery race
Flies in clear space
Straight to the sun;

Flies to the islands
Which on the sea
Seem to be floating
Gracefully free;
Where chorus on chorus
Shouting with glee
Over the meadows
Dancing we see.
In the clear air
Seeking their play,
Spirits are climbing
The hills far away;
Others are swimming
Over the sea,
Others soar free,
All toward life,
All to the fair, far
Loveliest star!

MEPHISTOPHELES He sleeps! Ye delicate, ethereal youths, 'twill do!
Ye have sung him sound asleep!
For this concert I am obliged to you.
No, Faust, you are not yet the man to keep
The devil fast! Let dreams of beauty flutter free
To plunge him in a sea of phantasy.
Yet to break the threshold's magic spell,
A rat's sharp tooth is needed. I can tell
I shall not conjure long; right near
A rat goes scuttling by; it soon will hear.
I, the Lord of rats and mice,
Of frogs and flies, of bugs and lice,
Command you promptly to appear
And gnaw that bit of threshold clear,
On which a drop of sacred oil was cast;
Here you come, hopping, hopping fast!
To work! The point which keeps me bound
Is on the outer angle found.

Another bite—that frees the door.
Dream on, Faust! till we meet once more!

FAUST *awakening*

Have I been deceived again to-day?
Did hosts of spirits, vanishing, make it seem
That the devil appeared in a lying dream,
And that a poodle scampered away?

IV
THE STUDY

FAUST   MEPHISTOPHELES

FAUST Who's knocking? Come in! Who's annoying me again?

MEPHISTOPHELES It's I.

FAUST   Come in.

MEPHISTOPHELES   It must be said three times quite plain.

FAUST Then come in!

MEPHISTOPHELES   H'm! That tone pleases me!
I only hope we shall agree!
To drive your moods away I appear
In the dress of a dashing cavalier,
With a coat of scarlet trimmed with gold,
A little stiff silk cape, a bold
Cock-feather in my cap, in pride
A long sharp rapier at my side.
And once for all I roundly advise
That you adopt this dress likewise,
So that with no restraint, set free,
You'll know what life can really be!

FAUST I'd feel, no matter what be my attire,
The misery of my life, its narrow way;
I am too young to be without desire,
Too old, too old merely to play.

What has the world to offer me?
Thou must renounce, renounce! That song
Is one which rings eternally
In every ear our whole life long,
And during life, throughout its course
Each hour sings till it is hoarse.
In horror only waking with the sun,
I could weep bitterly to see
The day whose course will not fulfill
One single wish of mine—not one—
But thwarts each budding joy that's sent,
By carping self-disparagement;
Through twisted views it keeps suppressed
The creative stir within my breast.
Even at night I'm forced, it seems,
To lie and worry on my bed,
But there I find no rest; instead
I'm terrified by wildest dreams.
The god who dwells within my breast
Can rouse my inner self at will,
Commanding my energies, and still
He cannot change my outer fate.
And thus existence is a burden,
Death I long for, life I hate!

MEPHISTOPHELES Yet Death is never wholly a welcome guest.

FAUST O fortunate the man in victory blest
Whose brow with blood-stained wreath is bound,
Who after a frenzied dance is found,
Close against a woman's breast!
O had I only expired in that hour
Of rapture, exalted by the Spirit's power!

MEPHISTOPHELES Yet someone did not drink one night
A certain brownish liquid—well, did he?

FAUST Spying it seems is your delight!

MEPHISTOPHELES   Though I am not all-knowing, much is known to me!

FAUST   When from that dreadful conflict drawn away
  By sounds of sweet familiar harmony,
  Fragments of childish feeling lingering in me
  Betrayed me with echoes of a happier day.
  Therefore I curse what seeks to cheat
  The soul with luring phantasy,
  Binding it with flattery and deceit
  Into this pit of misery!
  Cursed before all that lofty thought
  In which the spirit itself doth shroud!
  Cursed be the dazzling forms which sought
  Upon our senses to press and crowd!
  Cursed be all dissembling dreams
  Of fame and everlasting life!
  Cursed be all we flatter ourselves we own,
  As vassal, plough, as child and wife!
  Cursed be Mammon when with treasure
  He spurs us on to daring deeds,
  While merely for our idle pleasure
  Spreading the cushions for our needs!
  Cursed be the soothing juice of the grape!
  Cursed be love's ecstatic call!
  Cursed be hope! Cursed be faith!
  Yet cursed be patience most of all!

CHORUS OF SPIRITS *invisible*
  Woe! Woe!
  Thou has laid low
  The beautiful world
  By the force of thy blow!
  It totters, it crashes!
  A demigod smashes!
  We carry the fragments
  Into the void
  To bemoan and deplore

The beauty destroyed.
Earth-born,
Thou hast both power and might!
Create it anew
More glowingly bright;
In your breast let it spring.
A new life commence
With clarified sense,
Then, if you do,
New songs will ring!

MEPHISTOPHELES   These are my tiny agents.
Hark! They aspire
To counsel you wisely
To deed and desire,
To lure you out of this lonely state
Where the senses and life-force
Seek to stagnate!

Cease to play with your affliction then,
Which like a vulture feeds upon your life!
The worst of company would make you feel
Only that you are a man amongst men.
Yet I don't mean to thrust you back
Into the common pack.
I am not of the very great,
But if you'll take me as a mate
And go your way through life with me,
I shall willingly agree
To be yours on the spot.
I'll be your comrade to the grave
And if I suit—
I'll be your servant, be your slave.

FAUST But in return what must I do for you?

MEPHISTOPHELES You have a long time ere that note is due.

FAUST   No, no! The devil is an egotist,
And does not casually assist
Another person—just for God's sake too!
State all conditions plain and clear:
A servant such as you brings danger near.

MEPHISTOPHELES   Here I'll pledge myself at your command
To serve implicitly and without rest,
If when in the beyond we stand
You'll do the same for me at my request.

FAUST   The beyond fills me with small concern;
If you dash this world to fragments first,
The other may arise in turn.
Out of this earthly source my joy must spring,
And this sun shines upon my sufferings.
From both conditions could I separate,
Then let what will and can, appear!
Further, I do not care to hear
If in a future one feels love or hate,
Or if in any other sphere
There is a higher or a lower state.

MEPHISTOPHELES   On these terms you may well say yes.
Commit yourself. In days to come I mean
To show you all the arts which I possess;
I'll give you what no mortal yet has seen.

FAUST   What, poor Devil, could you give at best?
When was the human spirit in its striving quest
Ever understood by such a breast?
Yet have you food which never satisfies,
Red gold that like quicksilver flies,
Melting in the outstretched palms?
A game at which one never wins,
A girl though clasped within my arms,
Upon a neighbor casts her eyes,

The honor of a godlike aim,
Vanishing like a meteor's flame?
Show me fruits which rot ere gathered from the tree,
Show me trees which daily bloom anew!

MEPHISTOPHELES Such demands do not embarrass me!
Such treasure I can offer you.
But then a time will also come, my friend,
When you'll desire to feast in peace instead.

FAUST If ever I stretch upon an idler's bed,
Then let my doom descend!
If ever through lying flattery
You lure me into self-complacency,
If ever through pleasure you succeed
And trick me into feeling satisfied,
Let that day be my last!
This is my wager.

MEPHISTOPHELES　　　　　　　　　　　Done!

FAUST　　　　　　　　　　　Agreed!
If I should ever to the moment say,
"O stay! Thou art so fair!"
Clap me into fetters then and there,
And to destruction I shall gladly go!
Then may the death-bells toll,
Then from your service you are freed at last.
The clock may stop, the hands may fall,
My time will be forever past!

MEPHISTOPHELES Consider it well! I shall remember all.

FAUST You have the fullest right thereto;
This compact was not entered wantonly.
I'm a vassal if I persist in what I do;
Yours or whose—what difference can there be?

MEPHISTOPHELES To-day then, as your servant I will start,
And at your table carry out my part.
But one thing: merely a few brief lines to show,
In the event of life or death!

FAUST   And so,
You pedant, for something written do you call?
Have you no knowledge of man or his word at all?
Is it not enough that I must be
Bound by my spoken word eternally?
Does not the world, by all the streams of life compelled,
Rush on, and by a promise am I held?
Still this delusion lurks within each heart,
And who from this deceit desires to part?
Happy the man whose heart to truth doth yield,
No sacrifice will he be called to make;
Yet any piece of parchment written and sealed,
Is a spectre from which all men shrink and quake.
The word is dead before it leaves the pen,
But wax and leather dominate all men.
Spirit of Evil, what do you wish from me?
Brass, marble, parchment, paper—which shall I use?
Shall I write with chisel or quill? Come, choose!
Or perhaps a style? Decide—your choice is free.

MEPHISTOPHELES Why must you suddenly declaim
In this exaggerated way?
Any bit of paper does to-day!
Merely with a drop of blood inscribe your name.

FAUST If you are satisfied by such an act,
Let the farce continue to the end!

MEPHISTOPHELES Blood is a most peculiar fluid, my friend!

FAUST Do not fear that I shall break the pact!
The trend and aim of all my energy
Will be to carry out my vow. I see

I held my head too high; alas,
My proper place lies in your class.
The mighty Spirit cast me off in scorn,
And Nature closed her portals in distrust.
The thread of meditation has been torn,
Knowledge long has filled me with disgust.
Lost in sensual delight
The force of violent passions let us quell!
By impenetrable magic spell
Let miracles arise in sight!
Into the whirl of time we'll press,
The hurry-scurry of events! In full measure
Let pain and pleasure,
Worry and success,
Alternate as best they can;
Restless activity portrays the man.

MEPHISTOPHELES There is no goal prescribed, however high.
Nibble at everything as you may please,
Snatch at opportunity as you fly;
Whatever gives you joy, I hope agrees;
Only don't be bashful, just fall to.

FAUST Understand, once for all—pleasure is not the question!
To poignant joy and tumult I long to yield,
To exhilarating rage, enamored hate;
Nor shall my heart, from thirst of knowledge healed,
Henceforth to any sorrow bar the gate.
Deep in my self I will enjoy and find
The fate which is the lot of humankind;
Within my soul I'll grasp the worst and best,
Heaping their griefs, their joys upon my breast;
Thus to their selves my own self I'll extend,
To be destroyed as they are, in the end.

MEPHISTOPHELES O believe me, who for many a thousand year
Have chewed this hard and wretched fare,

No one from the cradle to the bier
Digests this bitter leaven anywhere!
Believe one of us—this entire parade
Only for a God was made!
He dwells in radiance forever bright,
Us into darkness he thrusts from sight,
While you! Be satisfied with day and night.

FAUST But that's what I desire!

MEPHISTOPHELES   A capital thought!
Still, one thing seems a trifle wrong;
Since time is short and art is long,
It struck me—if only you could be taught
With a poet to associate!
Let him give his thoughts free sway
And heap upon your worthy pate
The noblest traits he can display:
The lion's force,
The stag's swift pace,
The passion of the Italian race,
With northern constancy, of course.
Let him find out the secret link
Which binds nobility with craft and think
Up a clever, well-constructed plan,
To make you love wisely yet with youthful flame;
I'd also like to meet such a man,
"Sir Microcosm" would be his name.

FAUST What am I then, if I can never gain
The crown of humanity which from afar
Every sense is striving to attain?

MEPHISTOPHELES You will be in the end just what you are!
Get yourself a wig with curls a score,
Get yourself stilts a yard high or more,
You will be in the end—just what you are!

FAUST I feel that I have struggled to attain
The riches of the human spirit, all in vain;
Never when I sit down to rest,
Does fresh new strength well freely from my breast;
In height I'm not a hair's breadth more,
Not one whit nearer the Infinite than before!

MEPHISTOPHELES My dear man, you perceive this fact
Correctly in the ordinary light;
Far more cleverly we now must act
Ere the joys of life elude us quite.
The deuce! Of course your hands and feet,
Body and head are yours complete!
All I enjoy spontaneously—
Does that the less belong to me?
If for six stallions I can pay,
Are not their forces mine? And may
I not speed on as fresh and fine
As if four and twenty legs were mine?
Let all this brooding be—up then!
Come along with me into the world of men!
I tell you a fellow who speculates
Is like a beast on a barren strand,
By an evil spirit led round and round,
While about lies fair green pasture-land.

FAUST How shall we start?

MEPHISTOPHELES   We'll leave with speed.
What is this—a martyr's cell?
What kind of life is this to lead,
Boring yourself and the youngsters as well!
Leave such stuff to your neighbor, the ancient vat!
Why bother threshing straw? At that,
The best which you could ever learn
You dare not tell these lads in turn!
There, I hear one in the hall!

FAUST I cannot see him now at all!

MEPHISTOPHELES Poor boy, he had so long to wait,
He must not leave disconsolate.
Hand me cap and gown! . . . I can see
This costume will look rich on me!
He disguises himself in Faust's cap and gown

Leave it to me as I proceed!
Fifteen minutes is all I need.
Meanwhile prepare for a pleasant flight with speed.
Exit Faust

MEPHISTOPHELES *in Faust's long robe*
Scorn reason and science if you can,
The highest powers yet bestowed on man!
Through illusion and with magic arts
Let the lying spirit strengthen its hold,
Then, body and soul, I'll pin you down at last!
Fate gave to him a spirit wildly bold
Which drives him fast and still more fast,
And which with unchecked impulse sweeps him past
All earthly joys which he might hold.
I'll drag him through the wildest life,
Through meaningless inanity;
He'll wriggle, struggle, stick fast in his plight;
Because of his insatiate appetite,
Food and drink shall dangle in sight,
Before his greedy lips quite plain,
Yet he shall cry for sustenance in vain.
Had he not yielded to the devil to-day,
He would have perished anyway!
A student enters

THE STUDENT I came a little while ago,
And filled with deference am here,
A man like you to meet and know
Whom all men honor and revere.

MEPHISTOPHELES You please me by your courtesy!
                A man like other men you see.
                What experience do you bring?

THE STUDENT O please take me under your wing!
             I've come with courage, with faith untold,
             Youthful spirits, though not much gold;
             My mother scarce would let me go,
             Yet something worth while I'd like to know.

MEPHISTOPHELES You have selected the proper place!

THE STUDENT Quite frankly, I should like to quit!
             These walls and halls like endless space
             Do not attract me, I'll admit.
             It's all so cramped wherever one goes!
             No trees or green—no, not one bit!
             While class-rooms, with their chairs in rows,
             Make me lose hearing, sight, and wit!

MEPHISTOPHELES You'll grow accustomed none the less!
                No child will take its mother's breast
                At the start with willingness,
                Yet soon it feeds with utmost zest.
                Thus to wisdom's breast held tight,
                You'll crave your nurture more each day.

THE STUDENT I'll clasp her neck with real delight,
             If you will point me out the way.

MEPHISTOPHELES Ere you proceed, tell me if you can,
                What course of study you have found.

THE STUDENT I long to be a learned man,
             Possessing knowledge most profound
             Of heaven and the earth as well;
             Of nature and of science too.

MEPHISTOPHELES You're on the right track, I can tell;
                Let no distraction hinder you.

THE STUDENT With heart and soul I have begun;
             Yet speaking frankly, if I may,
             I'd like some freedom and some fun
             Upon a summer holiday.

MEPHISTOPHELES Conserve your time, for all too soon it flies!
                By system save your time is my advice.
                The first step that I recommend
                Is a course in logic to the end.
                There your spirit will be drilled to think,
                Cramped tight as if in Spanish boots; so **taught**,
                It then will circumspectly slink
                Along the path of stodgy thought,
                And cannot zigzag to and fro
                As a will-o'-the-wisp is wont to go.
                Many a day they'll need to make you believe
                That what you once could do as easily
                As eating, drinking, sleeping—you'll perceive
                Contains much more than one, two, three!
                To tell the truth the fabric of thought
                Is like some masterpiece a weaver wrought;
                A thousand threads one treadle guides,
                To and fro the shuttle slides,
                Subtly the unseen threads unite,
                Till one move knits a thousand tight.
                Up steps your philosopher to the fore
                Proving it must be so. What's more,
                The first was so, the second so,
                Therefore the third and fourth are so.
                If the first and second were not so,
                The third and fourth would not be so.
                All scholars laud this—but don't forget,
                Not one was ever a weaver yet!
                Who wants to study life and describe it rightly,

             First seeks to drive the spirit out; he thinks
             His hands have clasped the pieces tightly,
             But missing, alas! are the spiritual links.
             "Encheiresin naturae," is chemistry's cry,
             Mocking itself, not knowing why.

THE STUDENT I don't quite understand you, sir.

MEPHISTOPHELES Next time it will come easier,
             When you have learned how matters should be
             Reduced and classified properly.

THE STUDENT I feel confused by what you've said,
             As if a mill-wheel whirled inside my head.

MEPHISTOPHELES Above all else next you must turn
             To Metaphysics; manage to learn
             Its content thoroughly and attain
             What never was meant for human brain
             For what you can or cannot understand,
             An excellent word is right at hand.
             Be sure that during this half-year
             To punctuality you adhere.
             You'll have five hours when you start;
             At the bell be in your seat
             Prepared beforehand to repeat
             All your paragraphs by heart,
             So you observe the teacher quotes
             Only what the book is stating;
             Yet be as zealous taking notes
             As were the Holy Ghost dictating!

THE STUDENT No need to say that twice! I quite
             Agree how helpful this will be;
             All one takes down in black and white,
             One can take home contentedly.

MEPHISTOPHELES Select the subject which appeals to you.

MEPHISTOPHELES: Stand firm by your professor's word.
In general to words stick fast!
Then, into the Temple of Certainty,
Through safe, sure gates you'll pass at last.

THE STUDENT   For Jurisprudence I feel no call.

MEPHISTOPHELES   I do not blame you there at all;
I know this calling through and through.
Law and Justice eternally descend,
Direful as a disease which has no end;
They drag themselves from race to race,
And move insidiously from place to place.
Reason becomes nonsense, benevolence a pest,
Till you, the descendant, are sorely oppressed!
Yet of the law which is our inborn right,
Alas, that question never comes to light!

THE STUDENT   You make my own distaste more strong.
O lucky the man you help along!
Come to think of it, I'd like Theology.

MEPHISTOPHELES   I'd hate you to be led astray by me!
Where'er this science is concerned,
From false paths it is hard to keep;
In it such hidden poisons sleep,
From Medicine it is scarce discerned.
Here again, one man had best be heard;
Stand firm by your professor's word.
In general to words stick fast!
Then, into the Temple of Certainty,
Through safe, sure gates you'll pass at last.

THE STUDENT   Yet words must carry some ideas.

MEPHISTOPHELES   Right! But don't worry, for you'll find,
Precisely where the meaning slips your mind
A word at proper time appears.
With words it's easy to dispute,
For words build systems to the dot;
To words all faith one can impute,
From words one cannot steal a jot.

THE STUDENT My questions have detained you, sir,
          Still, I must bother you once more.
          Will you not say a trenchant word
          Of Medicine and its deep lore?
          Three years is such a little time!
          And heavens! the field is far too wide,
          One could much sooner find the way
          Had one a sign-post for a guide.

MEPHISTOPHELES *aside*

          I'm sick of this pedantic vein!
          I've got to play the devil again.
              Aloud

          The spirit of Medicine can be grasped with ease;
          Study the great and little world, my friend,
          To let it all go in the end
          As God may please!
          It's useless to roam about scientifically,
          Each man learns only what he can.
          But the man who grasps the opportunity—
          There is the real man!
          You have a rather fine physique,
          And are not shy; you'll find this true,
          That when you learn self-confidence
          Others will have faith in you.
          Above all learn to manage women: you'll see
          The endless Oh's and Ah's, which they
          Complain of everlastingly,
          Can all be cured in just one way.
          If you will be halfway discreet
          You'll have them eating from your hand.
          They will be led by your degree
          To think your arts all arts command;
          As a beginning, various spots caress
          Which others strove to reach for years:
          Her little pulse know how to press;

Then, with a fiery sidelong glance,
Clasp her round the slender waist
To see how tightly she is laced.

THE STUDENT   That's more like it! The where and how one sees.

MEPHISTOPHELES   Gray, my dear friend, are all theories,
And green the golden tree of life.

THE STUDENT   It seems the loveliest dream, I swear!
May I intrude again? Oh, might I dare
To tap your wisdom at the source?

MEPHISTOPHELES   I'll do all I can for you, of course.

THE STUDENT   I cannot tear myself away
Without requesting you to sign
My book of autographs. Please—just one line!

MEPHISTOPHELES   With pleasure!

                         He writes and returns it to the student

THE STUDENT   *reading*

"Eritis sicut Deus, scientes bonum et malum."

                         He closes the book reverently and withdraws

MEPHISTOPHELES   Follow my relative the snake and the ancient text;
In time, by your likeness to God you'll be wearily
    vexed!

                         Faust enters

FAUST   Where shall we go?

MEPHISTOPHELES   Why, where you please.
We'll see the small world, then the great;
With profit and delightful ease
You'll fool away time in this new state.

FAUST   Yet with this flowing beard of mine,
          I lack the social ease I need;
          This experiment will not succeed.
          In social life I cannot shine;
          People make me feel so small.
          I'll never be at ease at all!

MEPHISTOPHELES   Once gain self-confidence, all that will end;
          Then you will know how to live, my friend.

FAUST   How shall we leave, did you decide?
          Where are your servants, coach and pair?

MEPHISTOPHELES   We've but to spread this mantle wide,
          And it will bear us through the air.
          But upon this daring flight
          Take only luggage that is light.
          Some heated gas which I have found
          Will lift us quickly from the ground.
          If we're light, we'll quickly rise from here;
          Congratulations on your new career.

V

AUERBACH'S CELLAR
IN LEIPZIG

A carousal of jolly comrades

FROSCH   Will no one drink? no one laugh?
I'll teach you to make faces at me! To-day
You are just damp, limp chaff,
You always used to blaze away.

BRANDER   That's your fault; we get nothing from you,
No nonsense, no dirty jokes—what's one to do?

FROSCH   *pouring a glass of wine on his head*
There you have both!

BRANDER   You double-damned swine!

FROSCH   You wanted a joke—well, take mine!

SIEBEL   Whoever picks a scrap goes out that door;
At the top of your lungs, chorus, guzzle and roar!
Up! Hallo! Ho!

ALTMAYER   I'm done for! Come here!
Bring some cotton-wool! The fellow has split my ear.

SIEBEL   Only when the arches echo and ring
Do we feel how powerfully the basses sing!

FROSCH   Right! And out with him who takes offense!
A tara lara da!

ALTMAYER   A tara lara da!

FROSCH   Our throats are tuned, so let's commence!
He sings

The dear old Holy Roman Realm,
How the hell does it stick together?

BRANDER   A horrid song! Shame! A political song!
A rotten song! Thank God that you
With the Roman Realm have nothing to do!
At least I think it a capital thing
That I'm neither a Chancellor nor a King.
But since a leader we must select,
Come, then, a Pope let us elect.
You know the qualities which seem
To raise a man in our esteem.

FROSCH *singing*

Soar up, soar up, Dame Nightingale,
My love with a thousand greetings hail!

SIEBEL   No greetings to your love! That I won't allow!

FROSCH   A kiss and greetings to my love! You can't stop me
anyhow!
He sings

Lift the latch! the night is still.
Lift the latch! the lover wakes.
Draw the latch! for morning breaks.

SIEBEL   Sing on, sing on, just praise her as you will!
I'll have the laugh on you before you're through.
She made a fool of me—she'll do the same to you.
May a goblin lover be her fate!
He'll dally with her where the crossroads meet,
Some old goat, clumping home from the Blocksberg
late,

Prancing and dancing, "Good-night," he will bleat.
I tell you a fellow of real flesh and blood,
For that young hussy, is much too good!
No greetings will I ever send to that lass,
Unless with stones—to smash her window-glass!

BRANDER *pounding on the table*

Attention! Attention! All listen to me!
Sirs, you'll admit that I know how to live;
Some love-sick people are here, so I see
That a jolly good-night song we must give;
They have the right to expect that from me!
Attention! The latest song out! Come, sing!
A rousing chorus, with vigor and swing!

    He sings

In a cellar nest once lived a rat,
Whose paunch grew smooth and smoother;
For all he ate was butter and fat
Till he looked like Dr. Luther.
One night the cook spread poison 'round;
Then the world became as hot, he found,
As though love were burning his body!

CHORUS *shouting*

As though love were burning his body!

BRANDER

He ran about, he ran around,
Lapping up every puddle;
He gnawed and scratched the house throughout,
Naught helped him out of the muddle.
He writhed and whirled, his pain was such
That soon the poor thing suffered as much
As though love were burning his body!

CHORUS   As though love were burning his body!

BRANDER   By anguish forced into open day,

To the kitchen he ran scuffling;
On the hearth he fell and squeaking lay,
Most pitiably sniffling and snuffling!
The poisoner laughed with murderous glee.
"Ha, Ha! He's piping his last!" said she,
"As though love were burning his body!"

CHORUS   As though love were burning his body!

SIEBEL   How these dull louts do love this stuff!
I think it is a pretty sell
To give these poor rats poison enough!

BRANDER   You seem to like rats rather well!

ALTMAYER That bald pot-belly, fat and sleek,
The disaster makes him tame and meek;
In the swollen rodent he can see
His portrait lifelike as can be!

FAUST AND MEPHISTOPHELES

MEPHISTOPHELES First I wanted to bring you here
Into a jolly atmosphere,
To note how lightly life can slip away.
These people think each day a holiday;
With little sense and plenty of ease,
They spin about in circling trails,
Like kittens chasing after their tails.
As long as headaches they appease,
While the host gives credit, I declare
They live content and free from care.

BRANDER   From their curious get-up they appear
To be on a journey; it's quite clear
They've not been here an hour to-night.

FROSCH   Leipzig, to you! By Jove, the fellow's right!
Leipzig is a little Paris and gives tone to its people!

SIEBEL   What d'you take them for?

FROSCH   O let me be!
I'll get them drinking, then, no doubt,
I'll ferret their secrets as easily
As one can draw a child's tooth out.
They're of the nobility, that I can tell;
They look proud and discontented as well.

BRANDER   I'll bet they're fakers, on a spree!

ALTMAYER   Perhaps!

FROSCH   I'll trip them up—watch me!

MEPHISTOPHELES   *to Faust*
Though he has them by the collar, it is clear
Such people can't sense when the devil is near!

FAUST   Good-day to you, gentlemen!

SIEBEL   Thanks and the same.
In a low voice, looking at Mephistopheles from the side

What's the matter with his foot? Is the fellow lame?

MEPHISTOPHELES   Will you permit us to sit with you?
Your company will cheer us up in lieu
Of decent wine, which we can't get here.

ALTMAYER   Quite a fastidious person, I fear!

FROSCH   Perhaps from Rippach you started late?
Was it dark when you supped with Sir Hans to-day?

MEPHISTOPHELES To-day we travelled by and did not wait;
Last time we talked at length; he had much to say
About his cousins and, when he had done,
He sent his kind regards to everyone!
He makes a bow to Frosch

ALTMAYER *aside*
You got it there! He's on, I bet!

SIEBEL He's a sly dog!

FROSCH   Wait! I'll get him yet.

MEPHISTOPHELES Unless I'm wrong, did we not hear
A very well trained chorus singing?
Song must sound very fine and clear,
Back from these vaulted arches ringing!

FROSCH Perhaps you're an artist? Or am I wrong?

MEPHISTOPHELES O no! The power is weak though desire is strong!

ALTMAYER Give us a song!

MEPHISTOPHELES   Any number and very fine!

SIEBEL Be sure they're of a brand-new strain.

MEPHISTOPHELES We have just returned from Spain,
The lovely land of music and of wine!
He sings

Once upon a time there was a king
Who kept a large pet flea—

FROSCH Listen! Did you get that, fellows? A large pet flea!
Quite a neat little guest, it seems to me.

MEPHISTOPHELES *singing*
Once upon a time there was a king

Who kept a large pet flea,
On whom he lavished everything,
As if a son were he.
He called for his tailor; at this behest
The tailor promptly flew;
"Here, measure the lad for a coat and vest,
And measure him for breeches, too!"

BRANDER Don't forget, warn the tailor, ere he ceases,
To take the measurements to a hair!
For if he values his head, I swear
The breeches must fit without any creases!

MEPHISTOPHELES   In finest silk and velvet,
He was completely dressed,
With ribbons on his jacket,
And a cross upon his breast.
Prime Minister was his station,
An enormous star had he,
While at court each flea relation
Became a lord of high degree.

The courtiers and court ladies,
Tormented, were badly smitten;
The queen and her attendants
Were stung and sorely bitten.
They dared not flick and crack 'em
Wherever they itched at night,
But we'll flick and nick 'em
As soon as we feel 'em bite!

CHORUS *shouting*
Yes, we will flick and nick 'em
As soon as we feel 'em bite!

FROSCH Bravo! Bravo! But that was fine!

SIEBEL May this be the end of every flea!

BRANDER Nick 'em off with your finger cleverly!

ALTMAYER Hurrah for freedom! Hurrah for wine!

MEPHISTOPHELES In freedom's honor I'd gladly take a glass,
If only your wine were of a better class.

SIEBEL We don't want that from you again!

MEPHISTOPHELES I'm afraid the landlord would complain,
Else I would treat each worthy guest
To some of our cellar's very best.

SIEBEL Just bring it on! I'll take the blame!

FROSCH If the wine's good, we'll praise you—so make haste!
But don't hand out too stingy a taste;
For if as a judge I'm expected to shine,
I've got to have a good guzzle of wine.

ALTMAYER *aside*
As I suspected, they're from the Rhine.

MEPHISTOPHELES Get me a gimlet.

BRANDER Why, what for?
Your casks are not outside the door!

ALTMAYER The host has a tool-box right behind.

MEPHISTOPHELES *takes the gimlet; to Frosch*
What do you want to taste? Make up your mind!

FROSCH How's that? Have you got some of every kind?

MEPHISTOPHELES Each to his taste. The choice is free.

ALTMAYER *to Frosch*
Aha! You're starting to lick your chops, I see!

FROSCH   Good! If I'm to choose, for Rhine wine I call!
The Fatherland gives us the choicest gifts of all!

> Mephistopheles bores a hole in the edge of the table at
> the place where Frosch is sitting

MEPHISTOPHELES   Fetch me a little wax to make stoppers, quick!

ALTMAYER   Hm—that's just a juggler's trick!

MEPHISTOPHELES   *to Brander*
And you, sir?

BRANDER   Oh, champagne for me!
And highly sparkling let it be.

> Mephistopheles bores; meanwhile one of the others has
> made the wax stoppers and plugged the holes

One can't always abstain from foreign stuff,
As what is good is often hard to get;
A real German cannot stand a Frenchman, yet
He drinks his wines down willingly enough.

SIEBEL   *as Mephistopheles approaches where he is sitting*
I must confess I hate sour wine;
Give me a glass from a really sweet case.

MEPHISTOPHELES   *boring*
Tokay shall flow at once from the vine.

ALTMAYER   No, sirs, look me straight in the face,
You're making fun of us, I can see that you are.

MEPHISTOPHELES   With such distinguished guests? Oh, no!
That would be going a bit too far.
Only speak out! Hurry up though!
With what sort of wine can I serve you?

ALTMAYER   What's the difference? Any kind will do!

> After the holes have all been bored and plugged

MEPHISTOPHELES *making peculiar gestures*
> Mellow grapes the vine-stem bears!
> Crooked horns the old ram wears;
> Wine is juicy; of wood the vine;
> The wooden table too gives wine.
> Into the depths of Nature peer!
> Have faith, a miracle is here!

> Draw the corks and enjoy yourselves—don't stop!

ALL *together, as they draw out the stoppers and each fills his glass with the wine he has chosen*
> O lovely fountain rising to the top!

MEPHISTOPHELES Be careful though—don't spill a drop!
> They drink repeatedly

ALL *singing together*
> We feel as jolly as cannibals,
> As five hundred happy swine!

MEPHISTOPHELES Look! How well they feel, the rabble is free!

FAUST I should like to be leaving right away.

MEPHISTOPHELES Pay attention! Bestiality
> Will reveal itself in a striking display.

SIEBEL *drinks carelessly; wine spills upon the ground and turns to flame*
> Help! Help! Fire! Help! Hell's on fire!

MEPHISTOPHELES *addressing the flame*
> Be quiet friendly element!
> To the young men

> This time but a taste of hell-fire was sent!

SIEBEL What's this? Just wait! You'll dearly pay!
> You don't know whom you're dealing with to-day.

FROSCH Don't you try that trick a second time!

ALTMAYER I think we'd better quietly send him packing.

SIEBEL Well, sir? Is common sense so lacking
That you try this hocus-pocus pantomime?

MEPHISTOPHELES Keep still, old tub!

SIEBEL So you insult us too—you damned broomstick!

BRANDER Just wait! You'll get it fast and thick.

ALTMAYER *pulls a stopper out of the table; fire flies in his face*
I'm burning—I'm burning!

SIEBEL   It's witchcraft! Strike!
The fellow's an outlaw! Hit as you like!
                    They draw their knives and rush at Mephistopheles

MEPHISTOPHELES *with solemn gestures*
False words and images though fair
Change thoughts and scenery everywhere;
Be here! Be there!
                    They stand amazed and look at each other

ALTMAYER Where am I? What a lovely land!

FROSCH Vineyards! Do I see clearly?

SIEBEL   And grapes at hand!

BRANDER Beneath these arbors of different shapes,
See, what vines! See, what grapes!
                    He takes Siebel by the nose. The others do the same,
                    one to another, and raise their knives

MEPHISTOPHELES *as above*
Error, from their eyes loosen the band!
Mark you how the devil turns a joke.
                    He disappears with Faust; the young men separate

SIEBEL What's happened?

ALTMAYER   What?

FROSCH   Was that your nose?

BRANDER *to Siebel*
How? Is yours still in my hand?

ALTMAYER I tell you, fellows, that was a stroke
Which seemed to go through every limb!

Quick, get me a chair! My head begins to swim!

FROSCH But first do tell me what took place!

SIEBEL Where has he gone? If I can trace
That fellow, he'll not escape alive!

ALTMAYER I saw him . . . there,
Going out the cellar door, I swear,
Riding on a wine cask! . . .
My feet feel just as heavy as lead.
Turning towards the table

My! If the wine were flowing ahead!

SIEBEL It was all an illusion—a deceptive design!

FROSCH Yet I really seemed to be drinking wine!

BRANDER What about the grapes? Were they false, too?

ALTMAYER Who says miracles don't come true!

Delacroix inv. et Lithog.   Ch. Motte, Impr. Editeur à Paris.

SIEBEL: Help! Help! Fire! Help! Hell's on fire! . . .
. . . It's witchcraft! Strike!
The fellow's an outlaw! Hit as you like!

VI
THE WITCH'S KITCHEN

A large cauldron stands over the fire upon a low hearth.
In the steam that rises out of the cauldron various forms
appear. An APE sits beside the cauldron and skims it,
watching that it does not boil over. The HE-APE, with
the YOUNG ONES, sits near by and warms himself. The
ceiling and walls are covered with curious implements
of witchcraft

FAUST   MEPHISTOPHELES

FAUST   This frenzied, senseless witchcraft sickens me!
         Do you really promise I shall be
         Restored in such a frantic mess?
         From such a crone am I to seek assistance,
         And will her filthy slops remove no less
         Than thirty years from my existence?
         Pity me, if you know no better thing!
         Already hope is vanishing!
         Cannot Nature or a noble spirit find
         A healing balsam of any kind?

MEPHISTOPHELES   You're talking sense again, my friend! But look!
         There is a natural process to grow young.
         But that is written in another book;
         The chapter is a most peculiar one.

FAUST   I must know it.

MEPHISTOPHELES   Good! This process does not need
         Magic, gold, or medicine:
         Go to the pastures, there begin
         Straightway to hoe and dig with speed.

Keep your mind and self restrained
Within a narrow, humble sphere,
And by the simplest nurture be sustained.
Live with cattle as cattle live, nor think it ill
To fertilize yourself the land you till.
This is the best way, it is plain,
At eighty to grow young again.

FAUST　I am not used to that! I do not feel
Like stooping down to use a spade.
Such a narrow sphere has no appeal!

MEPHISTOPHELES　Then the old witch has to aid.

FAUST　But why just this old hag—that I don't see,
Why can't you brew the drink yourself for me?

MEPHISTOPHELES　What a pretty pastime! Why, I could make
A thousand bridges in the time 'twould take.
Not only art and science are needed here;
This work requires patience, too;
A tranquil spirit labors many a year,
Yet only time makes potent this strange brew.
And precious things alone we choose
As the ingredients we use.
The devil taught her how, 'tis true enough,
And yet the devil cannot make the stuff.
                    Gazing at the animals

See what a charming race is here displayed!
This is the man! That is the maid!
                    To the animals

It seems your mistress is out to-day?

THE ANIMALS　Out of the chimney she flew away,
Out of the house
To a carouse!

MEPHISTOPHELES　How long does her carousing require?

THE ANIMALS Until we have warmed up our paws at the fire.

MEPHISTOPHELES *to Faust*

What do you think of this dainty pet?

FAUST More absurd than anything I've seen yet!

MEPHISTOPHELES No, a conversation of this kind
Is the sort which appeals to my type of mind.
To the animals

Puppets of Abomination, speak out!
What sort of pap are you stirring and stewing?

THE ANIMALS A mess of thin soup for beggars we're brewing.

MEPHISTOPHELES You have many a customer, no doubt!

THE HE-APE *approaching and fawning on Mephistopheles*

O the dice swiftly throw,
Rich let me grow,
Let me rake in my gains!
Things are most unfair;
If I'd gold, I declare,
I'd also have brains!

MEPHISTOPHELES What a lucky fellow the ape would feel,
If he only had a turn at a roulette wheel.
The young apes, who have been playing with a large
ball, now roll it forward

THE HE-APE Such is the world:
Just like a ball,
See it rise and fall,
And roll and spin;
It rings like glass,
But soon breaks, alas!
It's hollow within.
Here bright it gleams,

There brighter seems,
Alive am I!
Dear son, I say,
Do keep away,
For you must die!
As 'tis made of clay,
Into pieces 'twill fly.

MEPHISTOPHELES What do you do with the sieve?
                              The He-Ape takes it down

THE HE-APE If you came here to thieve,
I'd know you right away.
                    He runs to the She-Ape and lets her look through it

Look through the sieve!
Do you know the thief?
Dare you name him to-day?

MEPHISTOPHELES *drawing near the fire*
What about this pot?

THE ANIMALS The simple sot!
Does not know the pot,
Does not know the kettle!

MEPHISTOPHELES Uncouth beast!

THE HE-APE Bring that broom at least,
And sit on the settle.
                        He motions to Mephistopheles to sit down

FAUST *who has been standing before a mirror all this time, now drawing near
and then drawing away*
What heavenly vision! What do I see
Within the magic mirror plain?
O Love, lend me your swiftest wings,
And bear me to her domain!
Ah, if I stay not rooted to this place,

If I but dare to venture near,
Then through a mist the imaged face
Of this lovely being seems less clear.
Can woman really be as fair?
Do I on this recumbent body gaze
As on a heavenly epitome?
Can this be found on earth?

MEPHISTOPHELES   Naturally
If a god torments himself for six whole days,
And then himself cries "Bravo" in the end,
Something clever must occur!
For this time look your fill, be satisfied!
I'll pick you up a darling just like her,
And happy the man who has the luck
To lead her as a bridegroom, home in pride.

> Faust continues to gaze into the mirror, Mephistoph-
> eles, stretching himself out upon the settle and playing
> with the broom, continues to speak

Here I sit like a king on a throne;
The sceptre I hold, I lack the crown alone.

THE ANIMALS *who have been making all sorts of curious gestures, bring a crown to Mephistopheles with much chatter*

O be so kind,
With blood and sweat!
The crown to bind!

> They handle the crown awkwardly and it breaks into
> two pieces around which they hop

'Tis done this time!
We speak and see,
Yet listen and rhyme!

FAUST *still before the mirror*

I'll go quite mad! O pity me!

MEPHISTOPHELES *pointing to the animals*

Even my head begins to shake!

THE ANIMALS   If luck is ours,
              To stir our powers,
              Thoughts we'll make!

FAUST   *as above*

        Oh, my heart begins to burn!
        Let us get away from here!

MEPHISTOPHELES   *in the same attitude*

        One must say this much: we discern
        They are true poets and sincere!

> The cauldron, which the She-Ape has neglected to watch
> until now, begins to boil over. There is a burst of flame
> which blazes up the chimney. With a horrible shriek
> the Witch comes flying down through the flames

THE WITCH   Ouch! Ow! Ow! Ow!
            Damnable beast! Accursed sow!
            Neglects the kettle! Burns her dame!
            Accursed beast!

> Perceiving Faust and Mephistopheles

        What doth appear?
        Why are you here?
        Who are you anyhow?
        What do you want now?
        May torturing flame
        Burn the marrow of your frame!

> She plunges the ladle in the cauldron and sprinkles
> flames over Faust, Mephistopheles, and the Animals.
> The Animals whimper

MEPHISTOPHELES   *reversing the broom which he holds in his hand and smashing about
                 amongst the glasses and pots*

        Crack! Crash!
        There lies the trash!
        There lies the glass!
        It's only a jest
        Keeping time, you ass,
        To your melodic pest.

As the Witch starts back, full of horror and anger

You know me then, you bag of bones? Abomination!
You recognize your master and your lord?
What hinders me from thrashing you,
Smashing you and your monkey horde?
Have you no more respect for the crimson coat than
    that?
Don't you know the long cock-feather in my hat?
Have I in any way concealed my face?
Must I even announce my presence in this place?

THE WITCH   Forgive my greeting so uncouth,
Yet I can see no cloven hoof;
Besides, your ravens—where are they?

MEPHISTOPHELES   This time you may get off this way.
For 'tis a long time, I'll admit,
Since last we met: and I can tell
That culture coating all the world so well
Has even tinged the devil a bit;
The Northern Phantom is no longer seen, and where
Do you find either claws or tail or horn?
While as regards the foot which I can't spare,
Since that would harm me socially, I've worn
Padded calves for many a year
Just like some other young men here.

THE WITCH *dancing about*

Reason and sense I wholly lack,
Since my Lord Satan has come back!

MEPHISTOPHELES   Woman! I forbid that name!

THE WITCH   Why so?
How has it harmed you, I should like to know?

MEPHISTOPHELES   That name was banned to story-books long ago,

Yet men are none the better, it's quite plain;
Freed from the Evil One, evil ones remain!
Call me simply Baron and we'll call it square.
I'm a cavalier like any other cavalier,
And lest you doubt my noble blood—look here!
This is the coat of arms I bear!

> *He makes an indecent gesture*

THE WITCH *laughing immoderately*

Ha! Ha! That's just what you prefer!
As shameless a rogue as ever you were!

MEPHISTOPHELES *to Faust*

My friend, watch what I say and do,
Learn how witches can be handled by you.

THE WITCH Now tell me, sirs, what you require.

MEPHISTOPHELES Some of that famous juice; but I desire
Only the oldest stuff, for you see
Time redoubles its potency.

THE WITCH With pleasure! Here I have a flask
From which I sometimes sip a drink;
Besides, this really does not stink;
I'll gladly pour you what you ask.

> *Aside*

Yet if he drinks it unprepared, you know
He cannot live more than an hour or so!

MEPHISTOPHELES He is a good friend, he will stand it well;
I don't begrudge your cellar's best to him.
Draw your circle, speak your spell,
Fill up a goblet to the brim.

> *The Witch describes a circle with fantastic gestures and places strange things in it; meanwhile the glasses begin to ring, the cauldron booms and makes music. Finally she brings out an enormous book and stands the Apes in the center of the circle, to serve her as a reading desk and hold the torches. She beckons to Faust to approach*

FAUST *to Mephistopheles*

Tell me what this is leading to—I've had enough!
These crazy gestures, this idiotic stuff,
All this vulgar trickery—
I know and hate it thoroughly!

MEPHISTOPHELES Fiddlesticks! Laugh at it if you can.
Don't be such a serious man!
As a doctor, she does some hocus-pocus too,
So that the liquid may agree with you.

He makes Faust enter the circle

THE WITCH *with great emphasis begins to recite from the book*

This you must know!
Make ten out of one,
Then let two go;
Make an even three,
Then rich you will be.
Discard the four!
Of five and six,
Says the witch, you'll fix
Up seven and eight,
Till it comes out straight;
And nine is one,
And ten is none,
This is the witch's one-times-one!

FAUST The hag's delirious, so far as I can tell!

MEPHISTOPHELES There's more to come, I know it well.
The book goes jingling on, page after page.
I've wasted so much time on it in vain,
As perfect contradictions will remain
Mysteries to a fool as to a sage.
The art is new yet old as it can be,
And has been used for ages past:
With three and one and one and three,

Error instead of Truth is cast.
They teach and jabber undisturbed;
Who cares to bother with a fool?
Most men believe, if they but hear a word,
That it contains a meaning as a rule.

THE WITCH *continues*

The lofty might
Of scientific light
Is hidden everywhere!
He who pays no heed
Receives it; indeed
Without any trouble or care!

FAUST What silly nonsense the creature drools!
My head will soon be cracked. Good Lord!
It seems to me I hear a horde
Of a hundred thousand chattering fools!

MEPHISTOPHELES Enough, O worthy Sibyl! Enough!
Bring on your drink and pour the stuff
Into the goblet quickly, to the brim!
My friend is safe, the drink won't injure him.
He is a man of great renown,
Who has gulped many a mouthful down.

> The Witch, with many ceremonies, pours the liquid into a goblet; as Faust lifts it to his lips a little flame leaps up

MEPHISTOPHELES Down with it promptly! Don't be slow!
It will do your heart good right away.
What! Hand-in-glove with the Devil you go,
Yet you shrink from fire in dismay?

> The Witch breaks the circle. Faust steps out

You must not stand still! Walk quickly, please!

THE WITCH I hope the taste you had agrees!

MEPHISTOPHELES If I can do you any favour, why, you might

Remind me of it on Walpurgis Night.

THE WITCH Here is a song for you to sing!
Its effect on you will be astonishing.

MEPHISTOPHELES Come quickly, let yourself be led about;
A proper perspiration must commence
For the potion's strength to flow both in and out.
Later I'll teach you to prize a noble indolence,
And soon with sense of pleasure you will know
How Cupid stirs and races to and fro.

FAUST Let me look into the mirror—just once more!
That form was so lovely I saw there before.

MEPHISTOPHELES No! No! The paragon of womankind,
Alive and real, you'll shortly find.
Aside

With this drink in your body you will see
A Helen in every woman instantly.

VII

A STREET

FAUST My little lady, may I offer you
My arm to see you home?

MARGARETE I'm not a lady, I'm not pretty—
I need no one to see me home!

She frees herself and goes away

FAUST What a lovely girl went there!
I've never seen one like her anywhere!
Such modesty, such sweetness—yet
Something pert in what she said.
As long as I live I won't forget
Those cheeks so flushed, those lips so red.
The way she shyly dropped her eyes,
Is deeply stamped upon my heart.
How short and sharp were her replies!
That was the most delightful part!

Mephistopheles enters

FAUST See here, get me that girl at once!

MEPHISTOPHELES   Why—
Which one?

FAUST   The one who just went by.

MEPHISTOPHELES That one? She just left the priest,
Who purged her from all sin—by talk at least!

Delacroix inv^t et Lithog.   Ch. Motte, Imp^r Éditeur, à Paris.

FAUST: My little lady, may I offer you
My arm to see you home?

I sneaked in right behind her chair;
She is an innocent for fair,
And goes to the confessional for naught;
I have no power over her sort.

FAUST But surely she is past fourteen!

MEPHISTOPHELES You're talking like a libertine,
Who craves each blossom that he sees,
Thinking all charm and virtue may
Be plucked by him with utmost ease.
It does not always work that way!

FAUST Most Reverend Master Moralist,
From preaching law and sense desist!
I tell you briefly and outright,
Unless that lovely little thing
Is lying in my arms to-night—
At midnight you and I will part!

MEPHISTOPHELES Consider it practically, indeed!
Fourteen days at least I need
Merely to sniff the way!

FAUST Had I but seven hours in all
I really should not need to call
The devil to lead that naive thing astray!

MEPHISTOPHELES You're talking like a Frenchman now!
Do not fret about it! Anyhow,
What's the use of rushing right through pleasure?
Your joy is never half as great
As when you dilly-dally at your leisure
And, with all sorts of nonsense, wait
To pet and mould the puppet well,
As many foreign stories tell.

FAUST I've appetite enough without that fuss.

MEPHISTOPHELES No scolding or nonsense—I'm serious.
That lovely child who just went past
Cannot be won by going fast!
You can't take her by storm; we must depend
On skill and strategy in the end.

FAUST Fetch me something the angel wears!
Take me to her place of rest!
Fetch me her garter as a token—
Fetch me the kerchief from her breast!

MEPHISTOPHELES That you may see how I, in your pain,
Try to serve with might and main,
I'll waste no time, but right away
I'll bring you to her room to-day.

FAUST Shall I see her—have her?

MEPHISTOPHELES   No!
She will be at a neighbor's when we go;
But meanwhile, left alone an hour or so,
You can imbibe her atmosphere and dwell
Upon the hope of future joys as well.

FAUST Can we go now?

MEPHISTOPHELES   No, it's still too soon.

FAUST Get me a gift for her this afternoon.
Exit

MEPHISTOPHELES Gifts already? Bravo! He'll win, I'm bound!
I know of many a lovely grove,
And many an ancient treasure trove;
I must be off and scout around.
Exit

VIII
EVENING

A small neatly kept room, MARGARETE braiding and tying up her hair

---

MARGARETE I'd give anything if I knew
Who that gentleman was to-day!
He looked so dashing, so handsome too!
He's of a noble family anyway,
That much I could plainly see,
Else he'd never have been so bold with me!
                    Exit   Mephistopheles enters with Faust

MEPHISTOPHELES Come in—quietly—but come in!

FAUST *after a moment's silence*
I beg of you—leave me alone!

MEPHISTOPHELES *prying about the room*
Not every girl would be so neat!
                    Exit

FAUST Welcome, dusky twilight, thou who dost shed
Upon this hallowed place thy gentle light!
Grip fast my heart, love's torturing delight,
Which on the dew of hope is fed!
Here peace and order breathe about me,
And deep contentment weaves a spell.
What abundance in this poverty!
What blessing in this little cell!
        *He throws himself into a leather armchair which stands
        beside the little bed*

O take me also, you who with open arms received
The joys and sorrows of a world gone by!
How often gathered about this father's throne,
Groups of children drew anigh!
Perhaps my little love came here as well,
With rounded childish cheeks; here she would stand
And, grateful for the Christ-child's gift,
Reverently kiss her grandsire's wrinkled hand.
I feel your spirit of order, O belovèd girl!
Which round about me seems to play,
Teaching you mother-wise from day to day
To smooth the tablecloth you lay,
To keep the sand so fresh beneath your feet.
O little hand so godlike and so sweet!
Through you this cottage becomes a veritable heaven.
And here!

He lifts one of the curtains of the bed

What a tremor of delight takes hold of me!
Here, in reverie how many a happy hour I'd stay;
Here, O Nature, you shaped as in a gentle dream
The angel born in this girl. There lay
The child whose soft breast slowly pulsed
With rising life; and here the fair design,
Woven in holy purity,
Created this fair image of the Divine.
And you! What led you here? What are you doing?
Why is your heart so heavy and so sore?
Why do I feel so deeply moved?
Miserable Faust! I know you no more!
Am I surrounded by an atmosphere of magic?
Driven here to enjoy myself, I find
That I am being dissolved in a dream of love!
Are we the sport of every gust of wind?
Suppose she entered at this very moment!
What a punishment for your wantonness!
Boasting fellow! Oh, how small you'd feel!

Crushed, you'd drop at her feet in sore distress.

MEPHISTOPHELES *entering*

Hurry! I see her coming!

FAUST Away! Away! I never will return!

MEPHISTOPHELES Here is a little casket, weighs a good bit;
For your sake, from its hiding place I've carried it.
Put it in the wardrobe—anywhere!
That's going to do the trick, I'll swear!
Inside I let some trifles lie,
Fine enough to catch another by;
But then a child's a child and play is play!

FAUST I wonder . . . should I?

MEPHISTOPHELES   Why question and delay?
You don't intend to keep the gems, do you?
May I suggest that if you do,
You cease this lustful longing, that you spare
Me any further trouble and care.
I really hope you are not stingy!
I wring my hands and scratch my head—

> He places the casket in the wardrobe and turns the key
> in the lock again

Quick, let's be off!—
To help you mould that sweet young thing
After your heart and will; instead,
You stand stock-still and stare and stare,
As if you were entering the lecture hall,
As if before you in the flesh
Physics and Metaphysics were standing there!
Come, let's go!

> Exeunt

MARGARETE *entering with a lamp*

It seems so close, so sultry now,

> She opens a window

And yet it's not so warm to-day.
It makes me feel, I just can't say—
But I wish mother were at home somehow.
From head to foot I'm shuddering!
Oh, but I'm a foolish, timid thing!

> *She begins to sing while she undresses*

There was a king of Thule,
True unto the grave,
To whom a golden goblet
His dying mistress gave.

At every feast he drained it,
He cherished it for years;
And every time he drained it,
His eyes were filled with tears.

When Death was close upon him,
He counted towns and land,
Then gave his heirs all riches
Save the goblet in his hand.

Surrounded by his vassals,
At the royal board sat he,
In the vast ancestral chamber
In the castle by the sea.

Up stood the hoary reveller,
And drained his last life-glow,
Then flung the sacred goblet
Into the tide below.

He watched it swaying, filling,
Sinking beneath the sea!
Then closing his eyelids softly,
Ah, never more drank he!

> *She opens the wardrobe to arrange her dresses and sees the little jewel-casket*

How did that pretty casket get in here?
I'm sure I locked the wardrobe door—that's queer!
My, it's handsome! I wonder what is inside.
Someone brought it as a pledge, maybe,
And mother lent some money on it. Why—
There on the ribbon hangs a little key!
I'd love to open it . . . I think I'll try!
What's this? God in Heaven! Look!
I've never, never seen such things before!
A set of jewels! Even a titled lady
Might wear these—on a holy day, what's more.
I wonder how the chain would look on me!
Who could ever own such jewelry?

> She decks herself with the jewels and steps before the mirror

If only just the earrings were my own!
One looks a different person right away.
What good are youth and beauty to you alone?
They are all very well as far as they go,
But beyond that there's not much to show!
Folk praise you, half in pity, so we're told.
All strive for gold, and in the end
It seems as if all things depend—
Ah, the pity of it—on gold!

IX

A THOROUGHFARE

FAUST lost in thought, walks up and down

Enter MEPHISTOPHELES

MEPHISTOPHELES By the depths of rejected love! By all the elements of
  Hell!
  If I only knew something worse by which to swear!

FAUST What's up? What stung you? Well, well,
  What a face! I've never seen one like it anywhere!

MEPHISTOPHELES I'd go straight to the devil
  If I myself were not a devil in fact!

FAUST You seem to have gone off your head from the way you
  act!
  Yet it becomes you to carry on like a lunatic!

MEPHISTOPHELES Imagine! The jewels I scraped up for Gretchen to-day,
  A miserable parson filched away!
  Her mother looking them over, it appears,
  Began at once to quake with hidden fears.
  That woman has the keenest sense of smell!
  She snuffles over prayer books time and again,
  Till sniffing at each object she can tell
  Whether it be sacred or profane.
  As for the jewels, she was soon aware
  That very little blessing could be there.
  "My child," she cried, "ill-gotten gain is sure
  To waste the blood, and for the soul's allure;
  We'll offer these to Mary, through whose grace

We shall win heavenly manna in their place."
But little Gretchen pulled a face and thought:
"What about the gift-horse? Why, it's clear
No wicked person ever would have brought
These jewels in this clever fashion here!"

Her mother called the parson, who came with speed,
Gave the gems a look of crafty greed,
And took the story in; then, at the end
He said: "Ah, that's a pious frame of mind!
Who conquers self, wins grace, you'll always find;
The Church has such a healthy stomach, friend,
And though it's gobbled many a land and state,
As yet it never overate!
My dear, good soul, the Church alone digests
Any ill-gotten treasure or bequests."

FAUST   That is a universal game,
Jews and Emperors do the same.

MEPHISTOPHELES   He pocketed the bracelet, chain, and rings,
As if they were mere trashy things,
And thanked them just as little, I dare say,
As though he took a basket of nuts away.
He promised them celestial gain; they sighed,
Were much impressed and edified.

FAUST   And Gretchen?

MEPHISTOPHELES   Sits there restless, overwrought,
Not knowing what she should or ought to say.
She dreams about the jewels night and day,
Yet more about the donor than she ought.

FAUST   I'm sorry that my darling has to fret.
Get her at once another set.
The first was not much anyway.

MEPHISTOPHELES   Of course to you it's all child's play!

FAUST   Hurry! Do what I said to do!
        Hang around her neighbor too!
        Fetch me new jewels in their place.
        Be a devil, not a milksop! Off now—race!

MEPHISTOPHELES   Certainly, sir, with all my heart, I'll run!
        Exit Faust

MEPHISTOPHELES   That love-sick fool would puff away
        The moon, the stars, the sun,
        Just to give his sweetheart fun!
        Exit

X

NEIGHBOR'S HOUSE

MARTHE *alone*

 May God forgive my dear old man,
 He really did not treat me fair!
 Off to foreign parts he ran,
 And left me moping in despair.
 I never worried him—not I!
 God knows I loved him, and with all my might.
    She weeps
 Perhaps he's dead! Oh, my! Oh, my!
 If I could only have it black on white!

MARGARETE *entering*

 Dame Marthe!

MARTHE   What is it, Gretchen dear?

MARGARETE My knees are almost giving way!
 I've found another box—look here,
 It's ebony! It was in my wardrobe to-day!
 And things much grander! See, a set
 Much handsomer than the one before.

MARTHE Now don't you tell your mother yet;
 Else she'll whisk them off to church once more!

MARGARETE Do see them! Oh! do look at them!

MARTHE *putting the jewels on her*

 Oh, you lucky, lucky thing!

MARGARETE Oh, dear! I cannot wear one to church,
Or on the street, not even a ring.

MARTHE Come over often to visit me,
And put on the jewels secretly;
Stroll before the mirror an hour or so,
And we'll enjoy ourselves; in time, you know,
There's sure to be a party—some pretext,
Where, one by one, you'll show the pieces without
fail;
At first the chain, the pearl-earrings next.
If your mother suspects, we'll invent some tale.

MARGARETE Who could have brought both jewel-boxes here?
There's something in it very queer.
A knock

Good Heavens! What if that be mother!

MARTHE *peering through the blinds*

It is a stranger. . . . Please come in.
Mephistopheles enters

MEPHISTOPHELES I make so free and come right in;
Ladies, excuse the liberty!
He steps back respectfully from Margarete

It's Mrs. Marthe Schwerdtlein I want to see.

MARTHE Here I am—what do you want of me?

MEPHISTOPHELES *aside to her*

I know you now—so that will do;
A distinguished visitor is with you.
Excuse me for having made so free;
I'll call this afternoon at three.

MARTHE *aloud*

Why, child, of all the funny things!
He takes you for a lady, dear!

Delacroix inv.t et Lithog

MEPHISTOPHELES: I make so free and come right in;
Ladies, excuse the liberty!

MARGARETE   The gentleman is much too kind, I fear!
            I'm just a poor young girl! The rings
            And ornaments are not my own.

MEPHISTOPHELES   Ah, but it's not the jewelry alone!
                 She has an air about her, a charming way!
                 I'm so delighted I may stay!

MARTHE   What brought you here? I wish I knew . . .

MEPHISTOPHELES   If only my tale ended happily!
                 I hope that you will not blame me:
                 Your husband is dead and sends his greetings too.

MARTHE   Is dead? That faithful soul! Oh, my!
         My husband is dead! Oh, I shall die!

MARGARETE   Do bear up, dear Dame Marthe—do!

MEPHISTOPHELES   Hear the sorrowful story through!

MARGARETE   I hope that I shall never love;
            Such a loss would make me grieve to death.

MEPHISTOPHELES   Joy has its sorrows as sorrow has its joys.

MARTHE   Tell me where he drew his dying breath.

MEPHISTOPHELES   He was buried in Padua close by
                 The church of St. Anthony; his bones now lie
                 In a cool eternal resting place,
                 A truly consecrated space.

MARTHE   Did you not bring me anything?

MEPHISTOPHELES   Oh, yes! A grave and great request:
                 Three hundred masses he wishes them to sing;
                 Otherwise my pockets are quite bare!

MARTHE   What! Not a lucky stone? No trinket there—

Which every workman stows away with care
In his sack, a keepsake till the end,
And would starve or beg, sooner than spend?

MEPHISTOPHELES Madam, it grieves me more than I can tell!
But truly he did not waste his little store;
He repented deeply for his faults as well,
Yes, bewailing his bad luck still more.

MARGARETE Oh, that men are so unfortunate!
Many a requiem I'll surely say!

MEPHISTOPHELES You are a lovable, worthy child;
You deserve to marry right away.

MARGARETE That's out of the question, though.

MEPHISTOPHELES If not a husband, meantime, perhaps a beau!
Heaven could not offer greater charms
Than to hold a darling like you in one's arms.

MARGARETE That's not the custom in this place.

MEPHISTOPHELES Custom or not, it's often the case!

MARTHE Please, sir, continue.

MEPHISTOPHELES   I stood by his side
At his death-bed, which was little more
Than manure and rotting straw; yet a Christian he died,
Finding he'd far greater debts charged to his score.
"How I despise myself," I heard him cry,
"Deserting my wife and trade to go to sea!
Ah, the memory is killing me,
O could she forgive me ere I die!"

MARTHE *weeping*
Dear, good fellow! I forgave him long ago.

MEPHISTOPHELES "And yet, God knows! She was more to blame than I."

MARTHE There he lied! What! At the brink of the grave—to lie!

MEPHISTOPHELES At the end his mind was wandering, there's no doubt,
If I am only half a judge! He said,
"There was no time for fun, nor could I stroll about;
First came children, then I had to earn their bread,
And all that this implies, with many a worry and care,
Yet not once was I allowed in peace to eat my share!"

MARTHE So he forgot my love and faith, as well
As all my drudgery both day and night!

MEPHISTOPHELES Not at all, he thought of it with all his might!
"When we set sail from Malta," I heard him tell,
"I prayed for my wife and children ardently,
And Heaven seemed to favor me;
Our vessel took a Turkish sloop whose hold
Was laden with the mighty Sultan's gold.
Then bravery its due reward obtained,
And, as was only just and fair, I gained
A liberally apportioned share."

MARTHE How's that? Where?
Has he hidden it? How?

MEPHISTOPHELES Who knows where the winds have carried it by now?
A pretty girl took him in tow,
When he was wandering in Naples without a friend;
Such love and faith did she bestow,
He felt the consequences till his end.

MARTHE The wretch! To rob his children! Then indeed,
All this misery and need
Could not change the shameful life he led!

MEPHISTOPHELES But don't you see—that's why he's dead!

And so were I in your place here,
I'd wear my mourning modestly one year,
But meanwhile for a new beau be looking round.

MARTHE Ah God! In this world never could be found
Another like my first! There scarce could be
A better-hearted fool than he.
Only he was too fond of roving about;
Foreign wine, foreign girls and vice,
Then, besides, the cursed dice!

MEPHISTOPHELES Come, come, things would have gone all right no doubt
If he had only really tried
To overlook as much as you did, on his side.
In a case like this, I swear 'tis true,
I'd exchange a ring myself with you.

MARTHE Go on, sir, you're making fun of me!

MEPHISTOPHELES *aside*
I'd best be off before this gets absurd!
She'd hold the devil to his word.
                    To Margarete

What about your heart—is it free?

MARGARETE Sir, what do you mean to imply?

MEPHISTOPHELES *aside*
You innocent child!
                    Aloud

                    Ladies, good-bye!

MARGARETE   Good-bye!

MARTHE One thing more before you go!
I'd like to have some proof to show
He died, was buried—when, where, and how;

I've always been one for proper form, you know;
I'd like to put a death-notice in the papers now.

MEPHISTOPHELES Yes, madam, by two witnesses, the truth
Is best confirmed; a clever youth
Is travelling with me whom I'll bring
To a notary to settle everything.
I'll go and fetch him.

MARTHE   Oh, yes, please do!

MEPHISTOPHELES Will this young lady be with you?
He's a fine young man, has travelled much,
And knows how to please the ladies, too.

MARGARETE Oh, the gentleman would make me blush.

MEPHISTOPHELES No king on earth would have the right!

MARTHE In my garden then, behind my house,
We shall expect you gentlemen to-night!

XI

A STREET

FAUST   MEPHISTOPHELES

FAUST How are the plans! Advancing? Soon complete?

MEPHISTOPHELES Bravo, I find you aflame! That's right!
Soon Gretchen will be yours; you'll meet
At neighbor Marthe's house to-night.
That woman was expressly made
To ply a pandering gypsy trade!

FAUST Good!

MEPHISTOPHELES   Something's asked of us as well.

FAUST One good turn deserves another.

MEPHISTOPHELES We've but to take a valid oath to tell
That her dead husband's limbs repose
At Padua in sacred ground.

FAUST That's clever! First we'll go there, I suppose?

MEPHISTOPHELES Sancta simplicitas! No need for that!
Swear, without knowing more than you do.

FAUST Unless you devise a better plan—I'm through!

MEPHISTOPHELES O saintly fellow! There you go!
    Is this the first time that your task
    Has been to bear false witness, may I ask?
    With brazen brow and dauntless breast,
    Did you not expound with power and zest
    Meanings of God and of the World—as well
    As of all creatures that within it dwell?
    Of Man, of all that stirs his heart and head,
    While if you probe the matter to the core,
    You must admit you knew but little more
    Than of this Schwerdtlein's death, when all's been said!

FAUST You are and remain a liar and a sophist too.

MEPHISTOPHELES Yes, did one not take a deeper view!
    To-morrow, in all honor, will not you
    Delude poor Gretchen and declare
    You love her with a love which is divine?

FAUST With all my heart!

MEPHISTOPHELES   Very good and fine!
    Then, eternal faith and love which surge
    Like a single overpowering urge—
    Will all that flow from your heart still?

FAUST Enough! When I am moved—it will!—it will!
    When into feeling I am whirled,
    And for this tumult of the senses seek a name,
    When I grope with heightened senses through the
        world,
    Striving for inspiring words, and call this flame,
    This ecstasy consuming me,
    Eternal! Unending!
    Is that just a devilish lying game?

MEPHISTOPHELES Yet I am right!

FAUST   Listen to me! Take heed,
I beg of you, and let me save my breath!
He who wants to prove he's right, and can talk you to
    death—
Is bound to succeed!
But come, I'm sick of all this useless chatter!
Since I must, I'll own you're right in this matter.

XII

A GARDEN

MARGARETE I'm well aware, sir, that you're sparing me,
Making me feel ashamed by doing so.
Often a traveller good-humoredly
Puts up with what he finds; indeed I know
My simple conversation never can
Appeal to so experienced a man.

FAUST One glance, one word from you appeals far more
Than wisdom and all worldly lore!

He kisses her hand

MARGARETE Oh, don't! How can you kiss my hand? Oh, dear,
It is so rough, so ugly, too!
Oh, what work I've had to do!
My mother is really too severe!

They pass out of sight

MARTHE You, sir, are always travelling to and fro?

MEPHISTOPHELES Business and duty keep us on the go!
We tear ourselves so painfully away
From certain places, yet we dare not stay!

MARTHE It's all very well when one is young and gay
To knock about the world year after year;
But when, as evil days draw near,
An old bachelor creeps to the grave alone—
No one fancies that, you'll own!

MEPHISTOPHELES   I shudder at the approach of such a fate.

MARTHE   Then, sir, think it over ere it is too late!
They pass out of sight

MARGARETE   Yes, out of sight is out of mind!
Politeness comes to you most naturally;
But surely many friends you find
Clever than I could ever be.

FAUST   Believe me, love! What passes for cleverness,
Too often is conceit and narrowness.

MARGARETE   I don't quite see.

FAUST   O why have innocence and simplicity
No knowledge of their sacred worth?
O could modesty and humility,
The highest gifts a loving Nature knew—

MARGARETE   Think of me sometimes, just a little while,
I shall have so much time to think of you!

FAUST   Are you much alone?

MARGARETE   Yes, our household's very small;
Still, it must be attended to.
We keep no maid; I do the cooking, sweeping and all
The sewing and knitting that there is to do.
Early and late I hurry so,
For in details my mother is—oh,
So exacting, you know!
Not that she really needs to scrimp this way;
We could afford to spend, better than others may.
My father left us quite a nice estate,
A house and garden near the city gate.
My life goes evenly on day after day.
My brother is a soldier of the King,

My baby sister, dead.
I had my troubles with that little thing;
Yet I would face it all again all I went through,
She was so dear to me!

FAUST   An angel, if like you!

MARGARETE   I raised her and oh, she loved me so!
My father died before she came; you know
We thought my mother lost; she lay
So weak and miserable, and day by day
She seemed to get her strength back—but so slow!
She really could not even try
To nurse the little mite, and it was I
Who reared her all alone
On milk and water—so she was my own!
In my arms or on my lap, the whole day long
She cooed and wriggled, growing strong.

FAUST   You must have felt a deep and pure delight.

MARGARETE   Yet many weary hours as well.
The little cradle stood at night
Beside my bed, and I could tell
If she but stirred, for I would wake!
Then I had to rise, to take
And lay her near me to be fed;
But if she'd not be still, get out of bed,
And pace the bedroom with the little thing,
Early to the wash-tubs hurry away,
Then watch the fire, do the marketing,
And ever on, to-morrow like to-day!
That's why sir, one's not always at one's best;
But food tastes better for it, so does rest.
They pass out of sight

MARTHE   Yes, women get the worst of it! They say
It's hard to make a bachelor change his mind.

MEPHISTOPHELES It's really up to women of your kind
To train us in a better way.

MARTHE Speak frankly, sir are you still fancy-free?
Has your heart not somewhere taken hold?

MEPHISTOPHELES The proverb says: One's hearth and wife
Are worth far more than pearls and gold.

MARTHE Did you not feel desire for anyone, I mean?

MEPHISTOPHELES People have been polite, everywhere I've been!

MARTHE Were you never seriously in love, I'm trying to say?

MEPHISTOPHELES Women should never be trifled with in any way!

MARTHE Oh, you don't understand!

MEPHISTOPHELES   I am so blind!
Yet this I understand—you're very kind!
They pass out of sight

FAUST Dear child, did you really recognize
Who came into the garden, and immediately?

MARGARETE Did you not notice? I lowered my eyes.

FAUST And you forgive the liberty
I took and my impertinence
As you came out of the cathedral door?

MARGARETE I was so upset! This never happened before!
No one ever spoke of me in an evil sense;
Oh, could he have seen—to myself I said—
Something improper, something bold in you?
For right away he takes it into his head
He can handle this wench the way he wishes to!
I must own up, something—I don't know why—

Was stirring in your favor from the start.
I felt so angry with myself that I
Could not be angrier with you in my heart!

FAUST Dear Love!

MARGARETE   Wait!

She picks a daisy and plucks off the petals one by one

FAUST   What's that for? A bouquet?

MARGARETE No, it's a game.

FAUST   How?

MARGARETE   You'll laugh at me! Go away!

She pulls off the petals, murmuring to herself

FAUST What are you murmuring?

MARGARETE *half aloud*
He loves me . . . loves me not.

FAUST Blessed Angel!

MARGARETE *continuing aloud*
Loves me . . . not . . . loves me . . . not . . .

Pulling off the last petal with pure delight

He loves me!

FAUST Yes, child! O let this flower's words
Be God's affirmation! He loves you!
Ah, do you understand what that means? He loves you!

He grasps both her hands

MARGARETE I'm trembling through and through!

FAUST O do not shudder! Let my eyes,
The touch of my hands reveal to you this,

This—that cannot be expressed!
To yield oneself completely, to feel
A joy which must be endless!
Endless!—The end would mean despair!
No, no end!—no end!

> Margarete presses his hands, frees herself, and runs off.
> Faust stands for a moment in thought, then follows her

MARTHE *coming forward*

The night draws on.

MEPHISTOPHELES   We must be on our way.

MARTHE I'd ask you gentlemen to stay,
But this is much too mean a place for you.
People here have nothing else to do,
No other thought it seems, day in, day out,
Than to tag their neighbor's steps and stare.
No matter how one acts, one gets so talked about!
And what of our young pair?

MEPHISTOPHELES   They flew up the path just there.
Playful birds!

MARTHE   He seems to take to her.

MEPHISTOPHELES And she to him. That's the way of the world.

XIII
A SUMMER HOUSE

MARGARETE runs in, hides behind the door, puts her
finger-tips to her lips, and peeks through the crack

MARGARETE   He's coming!

Faust enters

FAUST   You rogue! So you are teasing me!
If I catch you!

He kisses her

MARGARETE   *embracing him and returning his kiss*

I love you, dearest one, with all my heart!

Mephistopheles begins to knock

FAUST   *stamping his foot*

Who's there?

MEPHISTOPHELES   A friend!

FAUST   A beast!

MEPHISTOPHELES   It's time to part!

Marthe enters

MARTHE   Yes, sir, it's late.

FAUST   May I take you across the way?

MARGARETE   Oh, what would my mother say!
Good-bye!

FAUST   Must I go?
Then good-bye, my sweet!

MARTHE Good day to you.

MARGARETE   Till next we meet!
                    Exeunt Faust and Mephistopheles

Heavens! To think a man could so
Know everything there is to know!
I stand before him blushing red
And just say "Yes" to all he's said.
What a child I am! I cannot see
What he ever finds in me!
                    Exit

XIV
FOREST AND CAVERN

FAUST *alone*

Sublime Spirit, thou hast given me all,
All for which I besought thee. Not in vain
Didst thou reveal thy countenance in the fire.
Thou hast given me Nature for a kingdom,
With power to enjoy and feel. Nor didst thou permit
Only a visit of chilling bewilderment;
Thou didst allow me to peer deep into her breast
As into the heart of a friend. Before my eyes
Thou didst lead the ranks of living creatures,
Teaching me to know my brothers in the air,
In the deep waters and in the silent coverts.
When through the forest the storm rattles and rages,
Uprooting the giant pines which in their fall,
Crashing, drag down neighboring boughs and trunks
Whose ruin makes hollow thunder shake the hills,
Then thou dost lead me into a sheltering cave
And revealest me to myself and layest bare
The deep mysterious miracle of my nature.
And when the pure moon rises into sight
Soothingly above me, then about me hover,
Creeping from rocky walls and dewy thickets,
Silver shadows, phantoms of a bygone world,
Which allay the austere joy of meditation.
Now fully do I realize that man
Can never possess perfection! With this ecstasy
Which brings me near and nearer to the gods,

Thou gavest me this comrade whom I now
Cannot dispense with, though cold and insolent;
He lowers me in my own regard and can transform
Thy gifts to nothingness by one faint word.
Within my breast assiduously he fans
The flame of longing for that lovely image.
Thus from desire I stagger to enjoyment,
And in enjoyment, languish for desire.

Mephistopheles enters

MEPHISTOPHELES Come, come, have you not had your fill
Of this life yet? Can you enjoy it still?
It's all very well if you have tried
It once; but then go on to something new!

FAUST I wish that you had something else to do
Than to pester me when I am satisfied.

MEPHISTOPHELES There, there, I'll gladly let you be!
But you don't dare to say it seriously.
A comrade so unstable, rude, and cross
Is really very little loss.
One has one's hands full all day long,
Yet from the looks of him one cannot tell
What to say or what to leave alone.

FAUST Now he's struck the proper tone!
He bores me, yet he asks for thanks as well!

MEPHISTOPHELES Poor earthly creature! How, I'd like to know,
Could you have lived without some aid from me?
At least I cured you long ago
From torments of your phantasy.
To tell the truth if I had not been here,
You would have rambled off this sphere.
But what are you doing in these cliffs and caves,
Hunched up like a moping owl, alone?

What are you sucking like a toad which craves
Its nourishment from soggy moss and dripping stone?
A lovely pastime to dabble in!
Still the same old Professor, under your skin!

FAUST Can you not understand what fresh vitality
This living in the wilderness has wrought in me?
I do believe, if you could guess,
You'd be devil enough to grudge me this happiness.

MEPHISTOPHELES What a supernatural delight!
To lie in the night-dew on the mountain height,
Clasping earth and heaven in rapture! To inflate
Your being to a godlike state!
Burrowing through the earth with yearning urge,
Feeling in your heart the six-day creative surge,
Enjoying—I know not what—with power and pride
Next, the earthly self completely cast aside,
Flooding all with love's deep ecstasy,
And then the lofty intuition—
                    With a gesture

                              Hm—well, you see
I dare not mention what the end should be!

FAUST For shame!

MEPHISTOPHELES   You don't like it, eh? So you claim
The moral right to cry out, "Shame!"
Before chaste ears one cannot talk about
Some things which chaste hearts cannot do without.
Very well! I don't begrudge you the pleasure when
You lie to yourself a little now and then!
You cannot keep this up for long; of course
You are again distracted, and it's plain
If this continues it will force
You into depression, horror, or drive you insane!
Enough of this! Your sweetheart sits at home,

And life to her has a drab and dreary hue.
You never leave her thoughts at all,
She's overpoweringly in love with you.
First your passion rushed to overflow,
Like a brook when swelled by melting snow;
You poured it all into her heart and sigh
Because your little stream is running dry.
It seems to me, instead of playing king
Over these woods, your lordship could afford
To give the poor young silly thing,
For all her love and longing, some reward.
Time hangs so heavily upon her hands!
At her window, watching the clouds drifting over
The ancient city walls, idly she stands.
"O if I were a bird!" So runs her song,
Halfway through the night, the whole day long.
Sometimes she's happy—then she sighs;
Sometimes she simply cries and cries;
Then she is calm again, or seems to be,
But always utterly in love is she!

FAUST Serpent! Serpent!

MEPHISTOPHELES *aside*   Ha! I've got you now!

FAUST Infamous wretch! Away! Away!
Do not mention that belovèd girl!
Do not prick my tortured senses into pain
With craving for her lovely body again!

MEPHISTOPHELES What then? She thinks you've flown! I must confess,
That is what you have done, more or less!

FAUST Though I were far, I'm near to her somehow,
I'll never forget her, never lose her now!
I even envy the Body Divine
When her lips touch it!

MEPHISTOPHELES   Very, very fine!
          My friend, I've often envied you indeed,
          Those twins which 'midst the roses feed.

FAUST Begone, pander!

MEPHISTOPHELES   You rail, but I laugh! In truth
          The God who fashioned maid and youth
          Realized the noblest calling to be
          The power of making an opportunity.
          It really is a shame—however, we'll go!
          You should be going to your sweetheart's room,
          Not to your doom!

FAUST What though the joy of Heaven lies in her arms? What
          though
          I warm myself against her breast?
          Do I not always feel her woe?
          Am I not an outcast? a fugitive?
          A monster without purpose, without rest,
          Who like a cataract from rock to rock must leap,
          Then into the abyss with greedy anger sweep?
          Whilst she, with simple, childlike feeling,
          Lived in a cottage on an Alpine field,
          Where her modest home life was begun
          Within her little world concealed!
          And I, abhorred by God—
          O was it not enough, enough,
          When I embraced the rocks to blast
          Them into fragments at the last?
          Her peace I had to undermine as well!
          You claimed this victim, merciless Hell!
          Help, Fiend, curtail this time of misery!
          Let what must happen, happen without delay!
          Let her fate come crashing down on me,
          Let us sink together to our doom!

MEPHISTOPHELES Again he seethes, again he glows!
                You fool! Go in and comfort her!
                When such a pate no outcome knows,
                It thinks the end must speedily occur.
                Long life to the valiant everywhere!
                You're fairly well bedevilled otherwise!
                In all the world there's nothing I despise
                Like a devil in despair.

XV
GRETCHEN'S ROOM

GRETCHEN *alone at the spinning wheel*

My peace has fled,
My heart is sore;
I never shall find it,
Ah, never more!

My life is a grave
When he is not near,
And all the world
Is bitter and drear.

Oh! My poor head
Is so puzzled, so crazed;
My reason and senses
Are utterly dazed.

My peace has fled,
My heart is sore;
I never shall find it,
Ah, never more!

Just to see him I stay
At the window late;
Just to see him I hurry
Out to the gate.

His bearing, his manner,
Distinguished and wise,
The smile round his lips,
The flash of his eyes.

His speech, like the flow
Of some magical bliss,
His handclasp—and then—
Ah, then, his kiss!

My peace has fled,
My heart is sore;
I never shall find it,
Ah, never more!

My being goes out to him
Where'er he may be;
Ah, if I could clasp him
And hold him to me,

Then kiss him,
Then kiss him longingly,
Be lost in his kisses
In ecstasy!

GRETCHEN: My life is a grave
When he is not near,
And all the world
Is bitter and drear.

XVI
MARTHE'S GARDEN

MARGARETE   FAUST

MARGARETE Promise me, Heinrich!

FAUST   What I can.

MARGARETE Then tell me, what do you believe? Although
You are a good and lovable man,
You are not very religious, that I know.

FAUST Let that be, my child! You feel my love, is that not
true?
For those I love, I'd lay my life down too!
I would rob no one of his church or trust.

MARGARETE That's not enough! One must believe in it—one must!

FAUST Must one?

MARGARETE   If only I had some influence over you!
Neither do you revere the Sacrament.

FAUST I revere it.

MARGARETE But not with real feeling, I meant.
You've not been to Mass or confession for an age.
Do you believe in God?

FAUST   Who'd dare to say,
            "I believe in God"? Sweetheart, you may
            Ask any priest or sage—
            The answer which you would receive
            Would seem to mock the seeker.

MARGARETE   Then you do not believe?

FAUST Do not misunderstand me, blessed one!
            Who dares to name Him?
            Who can acclaim Him,
            Saying, "Yes, I believe in Him"?
            Experiencing Him everywhere,
            Who would dare
            To say, "I do not believe in Him"?
            The All-enfolding,
            The All-sustaining,
            Does He not enfold and uphold
            You—me—Himself?
            Does not the earth lie firm beneath?
            Do not the heavens arch above?
            Do not eternal stars ascend,
            Nodding with friendly light and love?
            Do we not look deep in each other's eyes?
            Does not a flow of feeling start
            Sweeping through you from head to heart,
            Weaving its eternal mystery
            Round you visibly, invisibly?
            Let its vastness suffuse and fill
            Your heart! When in this feeling wholly blessed,
            Then call it what you will!
            Call it Happiness! Heart! Love! God!
            I have no name for it!
            Feeling is all!
            The name is only sound and smoke
            Which fogs the glow of Heaven.

MARGARETE Yes, that's all very well and good;
           The Pastor says about the same,
           In other words, or so I've understood.

FAUST   All hearts in all places say
           The same, beneath the blessèd light of day,
           Each in his own words and way;
           So why not I in mine?

MARGARETE It sounds quite plausible when stated so.
           There's something just a bit crooked, though!
           You've no real Christianity!

FAUST   Dear child!

MARGARETE   It makes me miserable to see
           That you are in such company!

FAUST   How so?

MARGARETE   That man who goes about with you,
           I hate with all my heart and soul!
           In all my life, I never knew
           Anything could hurt me as a glance
           From his forbidding countenance.

FAUST   Darling, don't be afraid—you must not mind.

MARGARETE My blood runs cold when he draws near;
           Towards all others I feel kind.
           But much as I long to see you, dear,
           The sight of him fills me with uncanny fear!
           He is a scoundrel, that is plain to see;
           If I'm unjust to him, God pardon me!

FAUST   Such queer fish must also be.

MARGARETE I would not want to live with one like him!
When he by chance comes to the door,
He peers about so sneeringly,
Half-furious! One can see, what's more,
That nothing really interests him;
And on his brow it's written clear
He is incapable of love.
Ah, in your arms I feel so happy here,
So wholly yours, so warm, so free—
But near to him my heart contracts in me.

FAUST Intuitive soul!

MARGARETE   This overpowers me so that when
He meets us casually any day,
I feel I do not love you! . . . Then,
When he is near I cannot pray,
And this eats out my heart with pain;
O Heinrich, surely you feel the same.

FAUST There, there, it's just an antipathy!

MARGARETE Now I must go.

FAUST   Ah, shall I never rest
An hour quietly upon your breast,
Heart to heart and soul to soul, my own?

MARGARETE Oh, if only I slept alone!
I'd gladly leave the door unlatched to-night,
But mother sleeps so very light!
And were she to discover us,
I should fall dead upon the spot!

FAUST My darling, do not be afraid,
Take this little phial! Pour
Three drops into her glass—no more!
Nature with deepest slumber comes to aid.

MARGARETE   For your sake, what would I not do!
            It will not harm her if I should?

FAUST   Sweetheart, would I suggest it if it could?

MARGARETE   When I but see you, love, ah then I do
            Not know what power drives me to your will;
            Already I have done so much for you,
            That there is little left me to fulfill.

                    Exit.   Mephistopheles enters

MEPHISTOPHELES   The monkey! Has she gone?

FAUST   Have you been spying again?

MEPHISTOPHELES   I took it all in. I was most surprised!
                 The Professor was roundly catechized!
                 I hope it agrees with you. All girls appear
                 So very eager to find out
                 Whether a man is orthodox and devout!
                 They think: if he knuckled there—he'll truckle to us
                   here.

FAUST   You monster! Could you then not see
        How this soul, so pure and true,
        Imbued with the earnest faith she knew—
        Which meant to her salvation—
        Tortured herself with doubts, lest she
        Admit the man she loved bent for damnation!

MEPHISTOPHELES   You supersensual, sensual lover,
                 A girl is making a fool of you!

FAUST   Abortion of filth and flame!

MEPHISTOPHELES   Such an expert in physiognomy!
                 In my presence she feels she scarce knows what!
                 My little mask augurs some secret thought;

She's convinced I'm a genius of a sort—
Who knows, perhaps the devil himself!
As for to-night—

FAUST   What's that to you?

MEPHISTOPHELES Hm, I'll get my pleasure from it, too!

XVII
AT THE WELL

GRETCHEN and LIESCHEN with jugs

LIESCHEN Have you heard about Barbara, by the way?

GRETCHEN No, I'm seldom in company.

LIESCHEN   It's true, what they say!
Sibylle told me so to-day!
At last she's made a fool of herself for fair.
That's what comes of her grand air!

GRETCHEN What do you mean?

LIESCHEN   I'll explain it to you:
Whenever she eats and drinks—she's feeding two!

GRETCHEN Oh!

LIESCHEN   It serves her right!
How long she hung around that fellow! 'Twas a sight
To see them promenading up and down,
Toward the dance-place, through the town!
She had to be the first one everywhere;
And he, treating her to cakes and wine until I swear
She grew so vain about her pretty face,
She lowered herself and thought it no disgrace
To take his presents. Well, such a to-do!
Such kissings and goings-on!
Then the flower was plucked before one knew!

GRETCHEN Oh, the poor thing!

LIESCHEN   You need not pity her!
Whilst we girls from our spinning could not stir,
And nights our mothers kept us home,
She went gadding with her lover alone;
On the door-bench, in the dark corridor,
No hour ever was too late for her!
Now she'll have to hang her head,
And do penance in a sinner's shirt instead.

GRETCHEN Surely he'll marry her!

LIESCHEN   He'd be a fool! What for?
A clever chap like that has chances everywhere.
Besides, he's gone!

GRETCHEN   But that's not fair!

LIESCHEN If she gets him she had best look out!
The boys will snatch her wreath, while at the door
We will scatter chaff about.
                    Exit

GRETCHEN *going home*
How I once railed, in what a cruel way,
When some poor girl had gone astray!
I scarce found words enough to blame
And talk of someone else's sin and shame!
Black though it was, blacker it had to be,
Yet it was never black enough for me.
I blessed my stars, held my head high,
And now—now the living sin am I!
Yet all that drove me on to this—I knew
Only as sweet, only as true!

Delacroix inv.t et lithog.

Ch. Motte, Imp.t Lithrur.s Paris.

MEPHISTOPHELES: Thrust home!   VALENTINE: O God!

XVIII
RAMPART

In a niche of the wall is a shrine with a devotional picture
of the Mater Dolorosa. Vases for flowers are placed before it

---

GRETCHEN *putting fresh flowers in the vases*
Mother of Sorrows,
Bend down to me,
And look with pity and mercy on my distress.

A sword is piercing Thy heart,
And, racked by agony,
Thou art looking up to where Thy Son lies dead.

Thou hast turned toward the Father and Thy sigh
Ascends on high,
Because of His grief and Thy despair and dread.

But who can feel
The pain now torturing me
Unceasingly?

Why my heart's in anguish here,
All its longing, all its fear,
Thou and Thou alone canst know.

Whate'er I do, where'er I go,
How bitter the woe
Harrowing my breast!
And when I am alone again
I weep, and weep, and weep,
Breaking my heart in pain.

With tears the flowers beneath my window
Are watered bitterly,
As I gather them at daybreak,
To bring to Thee.

For when the sun with early light
Creeps into my little room,
It finds me up and seated on my bed,
Lost in misery and dread.

Help me! Save me from shame and death!
Mother of Sorrows,
Bend down to me,
And look with pity and mercy on my distress!

XIX
NIGHT

A street before GRETCHEN's house

VALENTINE *A soldier, Gretchen's brother*
When I'd be drinking with the men,
Where many fellows like to boast
About their pick of girls, and then,
Filling their glasses, drink a toast,
I'd sit in quiet unconcern,
Leaning on my elbows, and attend
To all their bunkum to the end.
Then smiling, stroke my beard and turn,
A brimming goblet in my hand,
And say, "Each to his taste! But where,
I ask you this, throughout the land
Is there a girl who can compare
With my own Gretchen? Out with it—say!
Who matches my sister in any way?"
Clink! Clink! "To her!" the round would fly,
And some "The fellow's right!" would cry,
"She's the flower of her sex, I swear!"
Dumb sat the braggarts one and all.
But now—oh, I could tear my hair,
And dash myself against the wall!
With a taunting sneer, nose in the air,
Each scamp has the laugh on me! Whilst I
Like a penniless debtor sit and sweat,
Flinching as chance remarks fly by

I could bang their heads together! And yet
I cannot tell them that they lie.

What's coming here? Who's sneaking up?
Unless I am mistaken, two appear;
If he's the one, I'll get him by the throat—
He'll never escape alive from here!

FAUST   MEPHISTOPHELES

FAUST As from the window of the sacristy, the light
Of the ever-living lamp is found
To flicker, then grow less and still less bright,
While darkness slowly closes in around,
So in my breast the dismal shadows close.

MEPHISTOPHELES Whilst I feel like a yearning cat which goes
Down the fire-ladders, slinking by,
Meandering along the fences, stealthily sly.
I feel quite virtuous, I do,
A bit thievish, a bit lustful too,
As down my limbs run thrills of pure delight,
Precursors of Walpurgis Night.
Day after to-morrow is the day; then, no mistake,
You'll know the reason why one stays awake.

FAUST Meanwhile will not the treasure rise in sight,
Which over there I see is glimmering bright?

MEPHISTOPHELES Very shortly you will know
The fun of lifting up a pot of gold;
I took a peep not long ago,
Some splendid coins it seemed to hold.

FAUST But is there not an ornament, a ring,
With which I can adorn my dear?

MEPHISTOPHELES It seemed to me I saw something
Like a string of pearls appear.

MEPHISTOPHELES: Quick, let's be off! It's time to disappear.

FAUST   Good! It hurts me if I have to go
        Without a present to display.

MEPHISTOPHELES   Pleasure for which you do not pay
        Really should not vex you so.
        Now that the sky with stars is brightly lit,
        You'll hear a very masterpiece of song.
        I'll sing her first a moral bit,
        The better to jolly her along.

He sings accompanying himself on the zither

        Katrinka dear,
        What are you doing here
        As dawn grows near,
        Outside your lover's door?
        I'd be afraid!
        He'll let you in a maid,
        But out a maid
        You'll not come any more.

        Beware! Beware!
        When once you're there,
        Why, then, my fair,
        Good night to you, poor thing!
        If you've self-respect,
        You won't select
        A scamp nor neglect
        To get the wedding ring.

VALENTINE   *coming forward*
        Whom are you trying to decoy? God's Element!
        You damnable, piping rat-catcher!
        First to the devil with the instrument!
        Next to the devil with the singer!

MEPHISTOPHELES   You've broken the zither in two. Now it's fit
        For nothing!

VALENTINE   Next there's a skull to split!

MEPHISTOPHELES *to Faust*
    Don't flinch, Professor! Just keep cool, stand pat!
    Follow as I lead—stick close to me.
    Out with your skewer quickly! See—
    You lunge!—I'll parry!

VALENTINE Parry that!

MEPHISTOPHELES   Why not? I'm only just commencing!

VALENTINE And that!

MEPHISTOPHELES   Of course!

VALENTINE The devil must be fencing!
    What's this? My hand's already lamed!

MEPHISTOPHELES *to Faust*
    Thrust home!

VALENTINE *falls*   O God!

MEPHISTOPHELES There—the lout is tamed!
    Quick, let's be off! It's time to disappear.
    Already they are shouting murder here.
    With the police I get on without fail,
    But the blood-guilt is a very different tale!
          Exit with Faust

MARTHE *at the window*
    Come out! Come out!

GRETCHEN *at the window*   A light! A light!

MARTHE *as above*
    They're shrieking, yelling and swearing . . . It's a
    fight!

PEOPLE   One is lying there already dead.

MARTHE   *coming out*
    Where have the murderers fled?

GRETCHEN   *coming out*
    Who's lying here?

PEOPLE   Your mother's son.

GRETCHEN   Almighty God! What have they done?

VALENTINE   I'm dying! That is very quickly said,
    More quickly done. Look here,
    Why do you women carry on? Instead,
    Listen to what I have to say—draw near!
        All crowd around him

    My Gretchen! You're still young, my dear,
    By no means smart enough, I fear;
    The fact is that you manage wrong.
    I'll tell you this in confidence: so long
    As you're a whore—since you've begun—
    Become one outright and be done!

GRETCHEN   My brother! God! What do you mean?

VALENTINE   Leave God out of this scene!
    I tell you what is past is past!
    What follows now will follow fast.
    You started secretly with one,
    Others will come once you've begun;
    And when you've had a dozen men,
    All the town can have you then.
    When shame into the world is born,
    She comes clandestinely 'midst tears;
    Then the veil of night is drawn
    Snugly round her head and ears;
    One could kill her! But when she grows,

And power arrogantly shows,
Brazenly she even flaunts by day,
Yet is no handsomer in any way.
The uglier her face becomes to sight
The more she seeks the broad daylight.

I see the hour drawing near
When all God-fearing people here,
From you, you prostitute! will turn away
As from a body in decay.
Your guilty heart will burn you through
When people merely look at you!
Never will you wear a fine gold chain,
Nor at the altar take your place;
Wearing a collar of the finest lace,
Never will you enjoy a dance again!
But in some corner, cast aside,
With beggars and cripples, there you'll hide.
Even though God forgive you, still
May you be damned on earth!

MARTHE   Commend your soul to God's good will!
          Must you take on the sin of blasphemy?

VALENTINE   If I could only reach your withered frame,
             You vile procuress—creature of shame!
             Ah, then I could have hope to win
             Pardon in full for every sin!

GRETCHEN   My brother! This is the agony of Hell!

VALENTINE   Dry those useless tears, I say!
             You dealt my heart a fatal blow
             When you flung your honor away.
             Now through the sleep of death, I ascend
             To God! A soldier to the end!
                         He dies

GRETCHEN: O God! O God!
If I could only free myself from the thoughts
Which float back and forth across my mind
Accusing me!

XX

IN THE CATHEDRAL

Mass with choir and organ. GRETCHEN amongst a crowd
of people. THE EVIL SPIRIT behind GRETCHEN

THE EVIL SPIRIT How different, Gretchen!
How different you were
When you came here to the altar,
So innocent, so chaste,
And murmured your prayers
From the worn befingered little book,
Half like a child,
Half stirred by God!
Gretchen!
Where are your thoughts?
And in your heart
What terrible crime?
Are you praying for the soul of your mother,
Which through your doing
Passed in sleep down, down into unending torment?
Whose blood is that staining your doorstep?
And beneath your heart,
Is not something stirring into life,
Tormenting itself and you with its ill-boding presence?

GRETCHEN O God! O God!
If I could only free myself from the thoughts
Which float back and forth across my mind
Accusing me!

CHOIR   Dies irae, dies illa
               Solvet saeclum in favilla.

               The organ is played

THE EVIL SPIRIT   The wrath of doom seizes you!
                  The last trumpet sounds!
                  The graves quiver and quake!
                  Out of the quiet ashes of death
                  Your heart is requickened,
                  Only to be plunged once more
                  Into the flames of torment!

GRETCHEN   If only I were away from here!
           I feel as if the organ
           Were robbing me of breath,
           As if the hymns were dissolving
           The very depths of my heart.

CHOIR   Judex ergo cum sedebit,
               Quidquid latet, adparebit,
               Nil inultum remanebit.

GRETCHEN   I cannot breathe! The pillars imprison me!
           The vaulted arch
           Presses down on me.
           Air! . . . Air!

THE EVIL SPIRIT   Hide yourself, Gretchen!
                  Sin and shame
                  Never remain concealed.
                  Light? . . . Air?
                  Woe upon you!

CHOIR   Quid sum miser tunc dicturus,
               Quem patronum rogaturus,
               Cum vix justus sit securus?

THE EVIL SPIRIT The Glorified turn
                 Their faces away.
                 The Pure shudder
                 At offering you their hands.
                 Woe! Woe!

CHOIR   Quid sum miser tunc dicturus?

GRETCHEN Neighbor! Help me . . . I'm fainting!
                 She falls to the floor in a faint

XXI

WALPURGIS NIGHT

The Harz Mountains. Vicinity of Schierke and Elend

FAUST   MEPHISTOPHELES

MEPHISTOPHELES Do you not long for a broomstick to-day?
I should like a goat both young and strong!
Our goal by this road still is far away.

FAUST This knotted stick suffices me so long
As I feel fresh upon my legs.
Why take the shorter cut? To me it seems
That creeping through this labyrinthine vale,
Before these rocky cliffs we scale
From which the spring continually streams,
Lends pleasure to a walk like this and zest!
Spring quickens the birches; one can tell
The fir trees feel its power as do the rest.
Why should it not affect our limbs as well?

MEPHISTOPHELES It does not touch me in the least!
My body still feels wintry and chill;
I long for frost and snow upon our path.
How sadly the imperfect disc of the red moon still
Is rising with belated glow;
So faint a light it seems to throw
That at each step one strikes a rock or tree.
Let me call a will-o'-the-wisp to me!
I see one burning brightly over there;
Ho, friend! Will you not aid us with your light?

MEPHISTOPHELES: Our goal by this road still is far away.

Why keep on flickering this useless flare?
Be good enough to guide us up the height.

THE WILL-O'-THE-WISP

Out of respect I hope I can subdue
My fickle nature and submit to you;
Usually we go at a zigzag gait.

MEPHISTOPHELES   Ho! ho! Does he try to imitate man?
Go straight, in the Devil's name!
Or I'll blow out your flickering flame.

THE WILL-O'-THE-WISP

I will adapt myself to you as best I can.
Here you are master. Bear in mind this fact:
The mountain is bewitched to-day,
And if you need a will-o'-the-wisp to light your way
You must not ask it to be too exact.

FAUST   MEPHISTOPHELES   WILL-O'-THE-WISP *in alternating song*

Since it seems we've been admitted
To these dream-like magic spaces,
Guide us nicely through these places,
So that soon we be permitted
In the vast and desolate regions.
Watch the trees like forest legions,
Passing by and swift descending,
While the cliffs keep bowing, bending,
And the rocks, long-snouted fellows—
How each snorts and how each bellows!

Over stones, through meadows growing,
Down rush brook and brooklet flowing.
Do I hear rustling? Do I hear singing?
Songs in which the heart rejoices,
Like those tender Heavenly voices
Which we love and, loving, hail

While faint Echo, like a tale
Of olden, golden days, is ringing?

Tu-whit! Tu-whoo! Not far away
Cry plover, screech-owl and the jay.
Did they remain awake to-day?
Does the long-legged, pot-bellied salamander
Through the tangled bush meander?
How the roots, like serpents winding
Out of rocks and sand dunes, linger,
Stretching tendrils like a finger,
Us to frighten—coiling, binding!
From the living, knotted gnarls,
Polypus feelers stretch their snarls
Towards the wanderer. Mice are scurrying,
Mice of thousand colors, hurrying,
Scuffling through the moss and heather!
While the fireflies are gleaming,
Flying, crowding, pushing, streaming,
Bewildered escorts, flocked together!

Tell me then, if we are waiting,
Or if onwards we are going?
All is whirling, rushing, blowing,
Trees and rocks are making faces,
Will-o'-the-wisps with arts and graces
Are augmenting and dilating.

MEPHISTOPHELES Come now, clutch my coat-tail tightly!
Here a middle peak is showing;
Whence, astonished, one sees brightly.
Mammon in the mountains glowing.

FAUST Through yawning chasms strangely gleams
A murky reddish tinge like break of day!
Into the deepest crevices it seems
To scent and pick its way!
There rises steam, there vapor drifts from sight,

Here out of mist and film flickers a glowing light;
Now trailing like a slender thread,
Now spraying like a fountain overhead.
Here for a distance it sweeps abreast
The valley in a hundred veins, to left and right,
While here, into a corner pressed,
Suddenly the streams unite.
Near by flashing sparks of light
Are scattering like golden sands.
But look—in all its splendid height,
Ablaze the rocky precipice stands!

MEPHISTOPHELES Does not Lord Mammon illuminate
His halls in splendor for this fête?
What luck you've seen it! Hush! I hear
The noisy guests are drawing near.

FAUST How the wind storm races through the air!
It beats upon my neck with blow on blow!

MEPHISTOPHELES Cling fast to the old ribs of the rock—take care!
Else you'll be hurled into the abyss below!
A heavy mist is darkening the night.
Hear the crashing through the woods! In fright,
Away the terrified owls flit.
Listen! The columns splinter and split
In the evergreen hall!
The branches crack and fall!
Down come the trunks with a terrible groan!
The roots, tearing violently, creak and moan,
As, snarled and tangled hideously,
Tree crashes heavily into tree,
While over the stormy wreck-strewn cliffs
Hissing and howling come violent winds!
Do you hear voices on the height,
Far away, then drawing nearer to me?
A frenzied song of sorcery
Is sweeping the mountain-crest to-night.

WITCHES *in chorus*

> The witches ride to the Brocken Horn,
> The stubble is yellow, green is the corn!
> The rabble is gathered awaiting the call,
> Aloft sits Lord Urian ruling them all.
> Here is the path, over stick, over stone;
> The he-goat stinks, and it————s the crone.

A VOICE Alone Old Baubo is coming now;
> She's riding on top of a farrow-sow.

CHORUS Give honor to whom all honors belong!
> Dame Baubo, come forward! Lead forth **the throng!**
> A good old sow and the mother atop!
> Witches follow her, neck and crop!

A VOICE Which way did you come?

ANOTHER VOICE   Over Ilsenstein crest!
> I peeked into an owlet's nest,
> She lowered and glowered!

ANOTHER VOICE   Oh, go to Hell!
> Why must you gallop like this, pell-mell?

A VOICE Ouch! But she grazed me passing by!
> Just look at the wounds that she gave me—oh, my!

WITCHES *in chorus*

> The way is wide, the way is long;
> How do you like this crazy throng?
> The broomstick scratches, the pitchfork pokes,
> The mother cracks and the little brat chokes!

WIZARDS *semi-chorus*

> We creep along like a snail in its house,
> The women before us; but if instead

They're on their way to the Devil's house,
Women are a thousand steps ahead.

OTHER SEMI-CHORUS

Such fine distinctions we don't make;
A woman a thousand steps may take,
But, much as she hurries to cover the ground,
A man arrives with a single bound.

A VOICE *above*

Ho there, from the Felsensee! Come up! Oh, do!

A VOICE *below*

We'd gladly climb the heights with you.
We've washed until we can't scrub more,
Yet we're as sterile as before.

BOTH CHORUSES   The wind is hushed, the stars die,
The melancholy moon hides in the sky.
While crowds of wizards whizzing by
Make sparks of sputtering fire fly.

A VOICE *below*

Stop! Stop! O don't let me be left!

A VOICE *above*

Who's calling from the rocky cleft?

A VOICE *below*

Take me with you! O please stop!
I have climbed three hundred years,
Yet I can never reach the top;
I'd like to be amongst my peers.

BOTH CHORUSES   A broomstick will carry you—so will a stick,
A pitchfork will carry you—a goat does the trick.
He who cannot raise himself to-day,
Lost forevermore must stay!

A HALF-WITCH *below*
> I've stumbled on till I'm half dead.
> How are the others so far ahead?
> For peace at home there is no chance,
> And here I never shall advance!

CHORUS OF WITCHES
> This salve gives courage to a hag,
> For a sail she takes a bit of rag.
> A ship is fashioned from a bough,
> He never will fly who can't fly now!

BOTH CHORUSES
> When you have sailed the summit round,
> Sink and trail lightly along the ground;
> You flock of witches, softly glide
> And cover the heath from far and wide.
>> They alight

MEPHISTOPHELES
> They crowd and jostle, they rattle and clatter!
> They hiss and they whirl, they bustle and chatter!
> They sparkle and spirt, they stink and they burn!
> A real witch-element as you shall learn!
> Hold on to me! Else we'll be parted in turn.
> Where are you?

FAUST *in the distance*   Here!

MEPHISTOPHELES   What! Thrust out of sight?
> I must ask them for house-room, asserting my right.
> Room! Sir Voland is coming! Rabble, clear the ground!
> Professor, take hold of me! Then with one bound
> Out of this crowd we will skip easily.
> It's even too crazy for one like me!
> Something shining with a curious glow
> Is drawing me to those bushes. Come, let's go!
> Behind them we will disappear.

FAUST Spirit of Contradiction! Onwards, lead!
       What a clever thought indeed!
       Climbing the Brocken on Walpurgis Night,
       To isolate ourselves upon this height.

MEPHISTOPHELES Look, what varicolored flames burn bright!
       Here is a club with quite a lively tone;
       In little circles one is not alone.

FAUST Yet to the heights I'd rather go!
       Already I see a whirling, smoky glow;
       To the Evil One crowds stream from every side,
       There many a knotty riddle might be untied.

MEPHISTOPHELES Also many a riddle knottily tied.
       Let the vast world rumble on and riot,
       Here let us house ourselves in quiet.
       Long ago 'twas known and plainly stated
       That in the great world, small worlds are created.
       See those young and naked witches there,
       And old ones, clever enough not to go bare.
       For my sake do be friendly to them all,
       The fun is great, the cost is small.
       Some instruments are being tuned up now;
       Damned twanging! Here one gets used to such a row.
       Come on! Come on! It has to be!
       I'll enter first and lead you in with me.
       I promise you something different in this place.
       What say you, friend? This is no tiny space!
       You scarce can see the end! Just think,
       A hundred fires in a row; they drink,
       They cook, they chatter, they dance, they kiss:
       Tell me, where is anything better than this?

FAUST To introduce us, will you devise
       A wizard or a devil's guise?

MEPHISTOPHELES Though nearly always I wear incognito,
                On gala days my orders I must show.
                A garter isn't any proof,
                Here they revere the cloven hoof.
                Do you see that snail which creeps about?
                With searching feelers just like eyes,
                It has already felt me out.
                Though I desired I could not wear disguise.
                But come! We'll go from fire to fire,
                I'll be the go-between—you be the squire.
                        To a few people who are sitting around some
                        dying embers

                Old gentleman, why sit so far away?
                I'd praise you if I found you placed to-day
                Well in the midst of all this youthful riot;
                At home one is alone enough in quiet.

    A GENERAL What faith can any man place in his nation!
                Although he squander all upon that land,
                With the people just as with a woman,
                Youth can always gain command.

   A MINISTER I sing and roundly praise the good old times.
                They've wandered far from all that's wise and sage.
                But the day we were in power—
                That was the veritable Golden Age.

   A PARVENU   We were not altogether stupid men,
                Though what we did oft was not right;
                Now the times are topsy-turvy,
                Just when we wished to hold the reins quite tight.

   AN AUTHOR   In these days who would ever read
                A book of sense and substance anyhow?
                As for the younger generation,
                They never were as impudent as now.

MEPHISTOPHELES *who suddenly appears very old*

> I feel that men are ripe for judgment day,
> The witches' hill a last time I ascend;
> Now that my cask is slowly dripping away,
> The world is surely coming to an end.

THE PEDDLER-WITCH

> Please, gentlemen, don't pass me by!
> Don't lose this opportunity!
> Look at my wares attentively,
> For many a curious thing you'll spy.
> Yet in my booth there's really naught
> Which somewhere else you will not find,
> And which at some time has not brought
> Grievous damage to mankind.
> There is no dagger here whose deadly aim
> Did not set blood a-flowing; furthermore,
> No goblet which at one time did not pour
> Consuming poison in a healthy frame;
> No jewel which did not seduce
> A lovable woman, no sword I lack
> Which has not severed a pledge of truce,
> Or stabbed an adversary in the back.

MEPHISTOPHELES Good Aunty, you're quite out of date!
> What's done is past, what's past is done.
> Get in a stock of novelties!
> By novelties only are we won.

FAUST If only I don't go mad in such a place!
> This fair keeps up at such a pace!

MEPHISTOPHELES The pack is crowding to the heights above;
> You are the shoved, although you think you shove.

FAUST Who is that?

MEPHISTOPHELES Watch her with care!
That's Lilith.

FAUST   Who?

MEPHISTOPHELES   Adam's first wife! Beware!
I warn you of her bright, fair hair,
Her ornament supreme! For this I know:
Once a youth is captured in that snare,
She will not lightly let him go.

FAUST An old and a young witch are sitting there,
Surely they have danced their share!

MEPHISTOPHELES To-day there is no rest for anyone;
Let's join them, come, a new dance has begun.

FAUST *dancing with a young witch*
Once I had a lovely dream,
There I saw an apple tree;
Two splendid apples there did gleam,
So up I climbed, they tempted me!

THE PRETTY WITCH

Apples have always tempted you
Since Paradise, long, long ago;
So I am overjoyed to know
That they grow in my garden too.

MEPHISTOPHELES *with an old witch*
Once I had a hideous dream,
There I saw a cloven tree;
It had a dreadful rent and yet,
Ugly as it was, it suited me.

THE OLD WITCH A hearty welcome to the Knight
Of the Cloven-Hoof—and may
He soon attend the cloven tree
Unless it frightens him away.

THE PROKTOPHANTASMIST

> Damned mob! How dare you be so indiscreet?
> Did we not long ago convince you then
> That spirits do not stand on ordinary feet?
> Yet here you come and dance like other men!

THE PRETTY WITCH *dancing*

> What does he want at our ball?

FAUST *dancing*

> Hm! he goes anywhere at all!
> He sits in judgment while the others dance;
> He talks of every step—if aught is missed,
> It's just as if the step did not exist;
> He's angriest whenever we advance.
> If you keep spinning round in circles still,
> As he does in his ancient mill,
> He will heartily approve of you,
> Especially if you listen to him too!

THE PROKTOPHANTASMIST

> I never heard the like! Are you still here?
> We've cleared the matter up! Quick, disappear!
> By no rules can this devil brood be daunted,
> We are so wise—yet Tegel still is haunted!
> How hard I worked to sweep this folly clean,
> And yet it's not. Outrageous! What do you mean?

THE PRETTY WITCH

> Shut up! Stop boring us! Oh, go away!

THE PROKTOPHANTASMIST

> Spirits, face to face I want to state,
> Spirit-despotism I won't tolerate;
> A spirit like mine won't be drilled.
>> The dance continues
>
>   To-day,
> I see there's nothing I can do!

Each journey gives me something though,
So ere I take my last, I hope to show
How I defeated the devil—and poets too.

MEPHISTOPHELES Down in the nearest puddle he will plump!
That is his way of seeking consolation;
He'll cure himself, with leeches on his rump,
Of the Spirit and of spirit domination.

To Faust, who has left the dance

Why did you leave that pretty girl
Who, as you danced, so sweetly sang?

FAUST Because—out of her mouth, while she was singing,
Suddenly a little red mouse sprang!

MEPHISTOPHELES Don't be so squeamish! Why, that's nothing at all!
Be glad the mouse was red, not gray.
Making love, who'd bother anyway?

FAUST Next I saw . . .

MEPHISTOPHELES   What?

FAUST   Mephisto, do you see . . . there—
Far off stands a child alone, so pale, so sweet!
She drags herself quite slowly from the place,
As if—as if she walked with fettered feet.
I must confess I seem to see
A likeness to my little Gretchen's face.

MEPHISTOPHELES That does no good to anyone! Let it be!
It's lifeless, an eidolon, a phantasy.
It is not wise to meet it anywhere.
Man's blood congeals before that frozen stare,
And he is turned to stone. One may suppose
That you have heard about the Medusa's head?

FAUST: Those are indeed the eyes of the dead
No loving hand did close!
That is the breast which Gretchen yielded me,
That the young form I loved so passionately!

FAUST Those are indeed the eyes of the dead
No loving hand did close!
That is the breast which Gretchen yielded me,
That the young form I loved so passionately!

MEPHISTOPHELES You gullible fool! It's just a magic play
Which each takes for his love in his own way.

FAUST What ecstasy! What anguish and despair!
From her glance I cannot seem to tear
My eyes away! How strange! Around her slender
   throat
There seems to run a narrow thread,
No wider than a knife's edge—and it's red!

MEPHISTOPHELES Yes, yes! That I likewise note.
She can take her head beneath her arm;
Perseus cut it off, yet did no harm.
Still your old desire for phantasy!
Come up that little hill with me;
It's as jolly there as in the Prater;
Unless I have gone off my head,
I really see a theatre.
What's going on?

SERVIBILIS Soon they will recommence
Another piece; 'twill be the last of seven.
They usually perform that number here;
A dilettante wrote the play,
And dilettanti appear in it to-day.
Excuse me, sirs, but I must disappear,
And like a dilettante, raise the curtain.

MEPHISTOPHELES On the Blocksberg, when I meet you dilettanti,
My heart rejoices. There you belong, that's certain.

XXII
WALPURGIS NIGHT'S DREAM
OR OBERON AND TITANIA'S
GOLDEN WEDDING

Intermezzo

THE MANAGER
> Here we shall repose at last,
> Mieding's sons so true;
> These old hills and sombre vales
> For scenery will do.

THE HERALD
> To have a golden wedding,
> Let fifty years fly by;
> Yet it would seem more golden
> Were quarrelling to die.

OBERON
> Spirits, have ye come to-day?
> Appear before me now,
> For your king and lovely queen
> Renew the marriage vow.

PUCK
> Here is Puck who spins around
> And marks time with his feet;
> Hundreds follow him about,
> Sharing in the treat.

ARIEL
> Ariel produces song,
> Clear as a heavenly bell;
> Many a fright it can entice,
> And pretty ones as well.

OBERON Couples, if you would agree,
       Listen to what we state!
       If you want to stay in love
       Quickly separate!

TITANIA If he scolds or if she's cross,
       Seize the pair, be bold!
       Take her to a sunny clime,
       Take him where winds blow cold.

ORCHESTRA TUTTI *fortissimo*
       Snout of flies, mosquito-bills,
       Relatives who are patricians,
       Frogs in moss, crickets in grass,
       These are our musicians.

SOLO Look, here come the bagpipes now!
       Soap bubbles, I suppose!
       Hear the schnecke-schnicke-schnack,
       Through each stumpy nose!

A SPIRIT IN EMBRYO

       Belly of toad, the spider's feet,
       And little midge's wings
       Do not make a little animal,
       Yet a little poem sings.

A YOUNG COUPLE Tiny steps and lofty leaps
       Through dew and breezy flights;
       Although you neatly trip along,
       You never reach the heights.

AN INQUISITIVE TRAVELLER
       Can this be a masquerade?
       Can I trust my eyes?
       Can Oberon, the lovely god,
       Be here without disguise?

AN ORTHODOX PERSON

Not a claw and not a tail!
He's really at this revel;
Though he is like the Grecian gods,
He may also be the Devil!

AN ARTIST FROM THE NORTH

The sketches I am tossing off,
Are trifles light as air;
For my Italian journey though,
In due time I prepare.

THE PURIST   Alas, misfortune led me here!
How indecent! Oh, how bad!
Amongst these witches only two
Are in powder clad!

A YOUNG WITCH   Powder, like a petticoat,
Suits gray and wrinkled faces;
So I sit naked on my goat
And show my body's graces.

A MATRON   We've really too much "savoir-faire"
To squabble with you here;
Despite your tender youth I hope
To see you rot, my dear!

THE LEADER OF THE ORCHESTRA

Snouts of flies, mosquito-bills,
Don't crowd around the nude!
Frogs in moss, crickets in grass,
Keep time, don't be so rude!

A WEATHER VANE *on one side*

Society! The sort one likes!
And brides—why, quite a few!
Bachelors, hm—I do declare!
What a hopeful crew!

A WEATHER VANE *on the other side*

If the earth won't open wide
To swallow this rubbish-heap,
Then I will give a nimble jump
And into Hell I'll leap!

XENIES   With tiny sharply pointed claws,
As insects we appear;
Satan, our dear papa,
We lovingly revere.

HENNINGS   Look! In crowds quite thickly massed,
All naïvely jest.
In the end they're sure to say
Their motives were the best.

MUSAGETES   I'd dearly like to lose myself
Amongst this witches' band;
Frankly, I find it easier
Than the Muses to command.

THE SO-CALLED GENIUS OF THE AGE

With the right people, one becomes someone!
Grab my coat-tails for salvation;
The Blocksberg, like the German Parnassus,
Has quite a broad elevation.

AN INQUISITIVE TRAVELLER

Who is that fellow strutting 'round,
With silly airs and graces?
He sniffs at everything he spies.
"He's on a Jesuit's traces!"

A CRANE   In clearest brooks I like to fish,
Likewise in muddy streams;
Thus one sees pious gentlemen
Consorting with devils, it seems.

A WORLDLING   Yes, everything may serve the ends
                       Of pious folks, I know;
                       Upon the Blocksberg they erect
                       Tabernacles in a row.

A DANCER   Another chorus? I declare,
                       I hear a distant strumming!
                       Don't worry! It is in the reeds,
                       The bitterns' steady drumming.

THE DANCING MASTER
                       How blithely they cavorted and
                       How deft the steps they took!
                       The crooked jumped, the awkward hopped,
                       And care not how they look.

A JOLLY GOOD FELLOW
                       The rabble hate each other so,
                       They'd kill, to say the least;
                       The bagpipe draws, like Orpheus' lyre,
                       Every savage beast.

A DOGMATIST   I'll not be falsely led astray
                       By doubts that critics see;
                       The Devil really must exist,
                       Else how could devils be?

AN IDEALIST   This phantasy within my mind
                       Is really much too glowing;
                       If all I see is really me,
                       Then silly I am growing!

THE REALIST   Living is a dreadful bore,
                       My grievance is complete.
                       This is the first time that I feel
                       Unfirm upon my feet.

THE SUPERNATURALIST
>   With utmost pleasure I have come,
>   Well pleased with all I view!
>   Since from the devils I foretell
>   The way of angels, too.

     THE SCEPTIC   They track the little will-o'-the-wisp,
>   Treasures they think are near!
>   As "doubt" is "devil" and "devil" is "doubt,"
>   With pleasure I appear.

THE LEADER OF THE ORCHESTRA
>   Frogs in moss, crickets in grass,
>   Dilettanti, damned unruly!
>   Snouts of flies, mosquito-bills,
>   Ye are musicians, truly!

THE ADROIT ONES   "Sans souci" this troupe is called
>   Of creatures most entrancing.
>   As we can't progress upon our feet,
>   On our heads we are advancing.

THE AWKWARD ONES We sponged on others just a bit,
>   Now God must help us out!
>   Since we have danced right through our shoes,
>   Barefoot we skip about.

WILL-O'-THE-WISPS Out of marshy swamps we come,
>   Whence first our family sprang;
>   In sparkling ranks we take our place,
>   A gallant, glittering gang.

THE SHOOTING STAR Down from the heights I darted fast,
>   Trailing sparks and fire;
>   Now I lie crumpled in the grass,
>   Who'll help to raise me higher?

THE HEAVY ONES   Room! Make room! On every side
                  The lawn is trodden down;
                  Here are spirits, spirits who
                  Have limbs so strong and brown.

          PUCK   Don't enter like young elephants,
                  With such a heavy tramp!
                  To-day the very plumpest one
                  Is Puck, the hardy scamp.

         ARIEL   If loving Nature or the soul
                  To you a wing discloses,
                  Then follow fast my airy trail
                  Up the hill of roses.

THE ORCHESTRA *pianissimo*
                  Veils of mist and drifting clouds
                  Aloft are shining bright;
                  Breeze in leaves and wind in reeds
                  Banish all from sight!

XXIII

A DISMAL DAY

Fields

FAUST   MEPHISTOPHELES

_____

FAUST   In misery! In despair! Despondent and distraught, she wandered pitiably for a long time over the face of the earth, and now she is imprisoned! Ah, to think that lovely, unfortunate girl should lie under lock and key, a prisoner, abandoned to appalling torment! Has it come to this! to this! . . . Treacherous, contemptible spirit, and you concealed it from me! Stand still— stand still! . . . Oh, you may roll those devilish eyes wrathfully around in your head! Stand still and defy me with your unbearable presence! Imprisoned! Lost in hopeless misery! Delivered over to evil spirits and to the pitiless judgment of men! And meanwhile you lulled me with insipid distraction, you concealed from me her increasing misfortune and allowed her to slide hopelessly into ruin!

MEPHISTOPHELES   She is not the first.

FAUST   Dog! Monster of abomination! . . . O thou Infinite Spirit, transform this reptile again into his dog-form! Transform him into the shape in which it pleased him so often to caper before me at night, rolling at the feet of a harmless wayfarer, hanging upon his shoulders if he stumbled and fell. Transform him into his favorite like- ness, that he may crawl upon his belly before me in the dust, that I may trample him underfoot, the outcast! . . . Not the first! . . . Oh, the sorrow, the pity of it all! Oh, it is more than any human soul can grasp! To think that more than one being should sink into this dark misery, to think that the first one who writhed in this death-agony should not have sufficiently expiated the guilt of all others in the sight of the Eternal Redeemer! The misery of this one soul pierces to the very marrow of my being; yet you can grin complacently at the fate of thousands!

MEPHISTOPHELES Once more we are at our wit's end, since we have reached the border line where human senses fail. Why do you seek our companionship if you cannot see it through? You wish to fly, yet you are not immune from dizziness? Come, come! Did we thrust ourselves upon you or you upon us?

FAUST Do not flash those greedy teeth at me like that! It disgusts me! . . . O thou mighty, glorious Spirit, thou who once deignedst to appear before me, thou who dost know my heart and soul, why dost thou link me to this infamous companion, who feeds upon suffering, and who gratifies his thirst upon ruin and desolation?

MEPHISTOPHELES Have you finished?

FAUST Rescue her or beware! An intolerable curse, a curse of a thousand years be upon you!

MEPHISTOPHELES I cannot loosen the bonds of the Avenger nor draw the bolts of his locks. Rescue her? Who caused her ruin? I—or you?
Faust gazes wildly about him

So you are seeking for thunderbolts? How wise that this power has not been vouchsafed to you miserable mortals! It is the way of a tyrant to destroy the innocent opponent who crosses his path when he seeks a way out of his dilemma.

FAUST Take me to her! She shall be free!

MEPHISTOPHELES What of the danger to which you will be exposed? Remember that blood-guilt—and from your hand—is still upon the town! Avenging spirits hover about the place where the victim fell, lying in wait for the return of the murderer.

FAUST This too—from you? Monster! May a world of death and destruction overwhelm you! Lead me there, I tell you! Set her free!

MEPHISTOPHELES I will lead you there: listen to what I can do! Am I all-powerful in heaven and on earth? I will befuddle the senses of the jailer; you get possession of his keys and lead her forth with human hand. I will keep watch! The magic horses are ready! I will carry you both away. This much I can do.

FAUST Up and away!

XXIV

NIGHT

A Broad Field.   FAUST and MEPHISTOPHELES dash
furiously across the field on black horses

FAUST   Why are they threading
Round and around the gallows-tree?

MEPHISTOPHELES   I do not know,
What they are doing
And brewing.

FAUST   They are soaring and sweeping,
And bending and bowing!

MEPHISTOPHELES   It's a witch-gathering!

FAUST   They pour a libation
And pray!

MEPHISTOPHELES   On! On!

Delacroix lith. et Lithog.   Ma Lay, Editeur, à Paris.

FAUST: Why are they threading
Round and around the gallows-tree?

XXV

DUNGEON

FAUST enters with a bunch of keys and a little lamp, and
stops before a small iron door

FAUST O'er me a long unwonted shudder falls,
The tragedy of life sweeps over me.
Here she lives, behind these damp, gray walls,
And yet her crime was but a fond delusion!
You do not go to her, you hesitate . . .
You fear to see her again! On! On!
Death draws nearer while you vacillate!

*He seizes the keys. The sound of singing is heard
within*

My mother, the harlot,
She put me to death!
My father, the scoundrel,
He ate up my flesh!
My dear little sister,
She laid all my bones
In a dark shady place,
Under the stones.
Then I changed to a wood-bird,
Fluttering and gay!
Fly away! Fly away! Fly away!

FAUST *unlocking the door*
She does not dream her lover is listening,
And hears the rustling straw, the clanking chain.

He enters

MARGARETE *hiding herself upon the pallet*
  Dear God! Dear God! They're coming!
  O bitter death!

FAUST *softly*
  Hush! Hush! I've come to set you free!

MARGARETE *throwing herself before him*
  Oh, if you are human—feel for me!

FAUST Hush, you will rouse the night-guard from his sleep.

MARGARETE *on her knees*
  Headsman! Who gave you
  Such authority?
  It's only midnight, yet you've come for me.
  Have mercy on me—let me live!
  Will it not be time enough at dawn?
                        She rises
  I'm still so young, so young!
  Yet I must die to-day!
  Once I was pretty, that was my undoing.
  My belovèd was near, now he is far away.
  My wreath's in shreds—the flowers scattered too.
  Do not take hold of me so violently!
  Spare me! What have I ever done to you?
  O do not let me beg in vain, I implore!
  No—I've never seen you in all my life before!

FAUST How shall I survive this anguish!

MARGARETE Look, I am wholly in your might!
  But let me nurse my child before I go.
  I held it to my heart all night;
  They took it from me, to worry me, I know,
  And say I killed it. That is what they say!
  I'll never, never be happy any more.

They make songs about me!
How wicked of people to make me cry!
An old, old story ends this way,
I wonder who knows why?

FAUST *falling on his knees*
One who loves you is lying at your feet,
To free you from the bondage of despair!

MARGARETE *flinging herself at his side*
O let us kneel and call upon the saints!
Look! beneath this very stair,
Beneath this threshold—look—look there,
Hell's bubbling and seething! And it seems
The Evil One,
In terrible wrath,
Rages and screams!

FAUST *loudly*
Gretchen! Gretchen!

MARGARETE *listening attentively*
Ah, that was the voice of my belovèd!
> She springs to her feet, and the chains fall off

Where is he? I heard him calling me!
No one shall interfere . . . I'm free!
I'll fly into his arms once more,
I'll lie against his heart as well!
He called "Gretchen!" He stood right at the door!
Amidst the howling and clapping of Hell,
Through all the wrathful, infernal scorn,
I knew the sound of his dear voice once more.

FAUST It is I!

MARGARETE   You! O say it over again!
> She embraces him

It's he! It's he! Where is my sorrow now? my pain?
Where is the terror of the dungeon? the chain?
It's you! . . . You've come to rescue me!
I'm saved!
Ah, once again I seem to see
The street in which I saw you first,
The little garden gay and bright
Where Marthe and I awaited you that night!

FAUST *pleadingly*
Come with me! Come!

MARGARETE   O stay!
Wherever you are I always love to stay.
She caresses him

FAUST Hurry! Away!
Unless you hurry now,
We'll dearly pay!

MARGARETE Can you no longer kiss? How's this?
Away from me such a little while, my dear,
Yet you've forgotten how to kiss!
Why do I feel so frightened here
In your arms enfolded, when
Once at just a word, a glance,
Heaven itself descended! Then
You kissed as though you'd stifle me!
Kiss me!
Else I will kiss you—see!
She embraces him

O pity me!
Your lips are chill,
And still!
Where is your love
Hiding?
Who has done me this cruel wrong?
She turns away from him

FAUST   Come! Follow me! Sweetheart, be strong!
A thousand times more lovingly I'll kiss,
If you come with me now! I only ask you this!

MARGARETE   *coming nearer*
And is it you? Really, really you?

FAUST   It is I! O come with me!

MARGARETE   You snapped my chain,
O take me on your lap again!
How is it that you do not shrink from me?
Do you know, belovèd, whom you are setting free?

FAUST   Come, come! The depths of night are yielding fast!

MARGARETE   I put my mother to death;
I drowned my child.
Was it not a gift to you and to me?
And you, too! . . . It's you! . . . I scarce believe it!
Give me your hand! This is no dream!
Your dear, dear hand! . . . Ah, it's damp! How can
that be?
Wipe it off! It would seem
As if blood were on it.
O God! What have you done!
Put that sword away,
I beg of you!

FAUST   O let the past be past,
You'll kill me unless you do!

MARGARETE   No, no, belovèd, you must survive!
I will describe to you with care
The graves to-morrow to prepare:
The best place you must give to mother,
And close beside her lay my brother.
Somewhere to one side let me stay—

But only not too far away!
The little one at my right breast,
For no one else will ever lie near.
O what sweet, what sacred joy
It was to nestle to you, dear!
But that will never be again.
I feel I have to force myself on you,
As if you pushed me back with might and main!
And yet it's really, really you!
And you seem so kind, so true.

FAUST If you feel it's really I—then come!

MARGARETE Out there?

FAUST   Into freedom!

MARGARETE If the grave you'll prepare,
If death's lurking there,
Then come! From here to eternal rest—
Otherwise, not a step with you!
You're going? O Heinrich, if I could go too!

FAUST You can! If you will only try! The door is open wide.

MARGARETE There is no hope for me, I dare not step outside.
What use to fly? They'd only hound me out,
Just as before!
O what misery to beg and roam about,
With an evil conscience, furthermore!
What misery to wander on each day;
And they would catch me anyway!

FAUST I'll stay with you.

MARGARETE Hurry! Hurry!
Save your poor child!
Be off! Keep closely to the path

Up by the brook . . .
Across . . . across . . . where the old bridge stood
In the heart of the wood!
To the left . . . where the plank lies
In the pool! . . . Seize it—quick!
It's trying to rise!
Save it . . . See! . . . See,
It's struggling still!

FAUST   Come to yourself!
One step, dear, then you are free!

MARGARETE   If only we were past that hill!
My mother sits there, on top of a stone,
Down my spine creeps a chill of dread!
My mother sits there, on top of a stone,
Wagging and wagging her head.
She can't nod, she can't wink, her head's heavy and
        sore,
She has slept so long she will wake no more.
She slept so that we could have joy always!
Oh, those were such happy, happy days!

FAUST   Here words, here prayers are no avail! I see
That I must try to carry you away.

MARGARETE   Do not grip me so murderously!
Let me go! I will endure no force, I say!
Once I did everything for love of you.

FAUST   The day is dawning! Love—dear love!

MARGARETE   Dawn? Yes, it is the dawn! The last day hurries on its
        way.
Why, this should have been my wedding day!
Tell no one you already were with Gretchen—
Alas! My poor wreath! . . .

All's over now! . . . Once more quite plain,
We shall see each other again,
But it will not be at a dance.
The crowd is gathering, silent as in a trance,
The streets, the square,
Scarce hold them there.
The death bells are tolling, the rod is broken,
How they seize me, how they bind me tight!
Now I'm shoved to the block, now the knife quivers in
    fright
Over everyone's neck as it quivers o'er mine;
And the world lies still as the grave!

FAUST O that I had never been born!

                  Mephistopheles appears outside

MEPHISTOPHELES Away! Else both of you are lost! Away!
Such useless chatter! Talk, talk and delay!
My horses are shivering and shaking!
Dawn is breaking!

MARGARETE What's rising out of the ground? That face!
Send him away! It is he! it is he!
What does he want in this holy place?
Ah—he wants me!

FAUST You shall live!

MARGARETE Judgment of God! I give myself up to you!

MEPHISTOPHELES *to Faust*
Come, come! I'll desert you both unless you do!

MARGARETE Father, I am thine! Save me!
Holy angels, sacred hosts, appear,
Guard me, close around me here!
Heinrich! I am aghast at you!

MEPHISTOPHELES: Away! Else both of you are lost! Away!
Such useless chatter! Talk, talk and delay!
My horses are shivering and shaking!
Dawn is breaking!

MEPHISTOPHELES She is doomed!

VOICE FROM ABOVE   Is saved!

MEPHISTOPHELES *to Faust*   Come, be quick!
                                   He disappears with Faust

      A VOICE *from within, dying away*
                  Belovèd . . . Belovèd!